THE COVENT GARDEN ALBUM

THE COVENT GARDEN ALBUM

250 YEARS OF THEATRE, OPERA AND BALLET

LORD DROGHEDA
KEN DAVISON
ANDREW WHEATCROFT

ROUTLEDGE & KEGAN PAUL
LONDON AND HENLEY

FIRST PUBLISHED IN 1981
BY ROUTLEDGE & KEGAN PAUL LTD
39 STORE STREET, LONDON WC1E 7DD AND
BROADWAY HOUSE, NEWTOWN ROAD, HENLEY ON THAMES, OXON RG9 1EN

DESIGNED BY LOGOS DESIGN
SET IN MONOPHOTO GARAMOND 156
AND PRINTED IN GREAT BRITAIN BY BAS PRINTERS LIMITED,
OVER WALLOP, HAMPSHIRE
© THE EARL OF DROGHEDA, KENSINGTON DAVISON AND THE WESSELL PRESS 1981

BRITISH LIBRARY CATALOGUING IN PUBLICATION DATA

DROGHEDA, CHARLES GARRETT PONSONBY MOORE,
EARL OF
THE COVENT GARDEN ALBUM.
I. TITLE   II. DAVISON, KEN
III. WHEATCROFT, ANDREW
782.1′ 09421′ 32   PN2596.L7R

ISBN 0-7100-0880-5

CONTENTS

PREFACE

IT WAS THE CUSTOM during the 1930s for programmes at the Royal Opera House to bear the slogan: 'The world's greatest theatre.' It is not the purpose of this book to make that claim, but it is undeniable that the stage at Covent Garden has seen some supreme performances in its long history, in the three arts of theatre, opera and ballet.

WE HAVE SOUGHT not to present a history of the theatre and its productions – an enterprise which would require a series of substantial volumes – but an evocation of its past and present. We have chosen to use, for the most part, visual images rather than the written word, partly because they are more immediate, but partly also because we wished to portray the theatre by means of a family album. In an album, the arrangement and contents are subjective, making no claim to tell every side of the story. Family albums are more concerned with success and happiness rather than with failure and despair, and so it is with our *Covent Garden Album*.

IN THESE PAGES we have sought to show some of the great artists who have appeared upon its boards, the landmarks of its history, and to indicate something of the role it has come to assume both in the culture of the nation and internationally. It appears at this moment in celebration of 250 years of theatre, opera and ballet upon this site, and in tribute to an institution which can have few rivals.

GD – KD – AW

ACKNOWLEDGMENTS

THE MATERIAL for the history of the theatres in Covent Garden is vast—a detailed archive in the Royal Opera House itself, and an even larger holding in the Theatre Museum at present in the Victoria and Albert Museum. It is to the staffs of these two institutions that the authors owe a considerable debt of gratitude. To Francesca Franchi, of the Royal Opera House archives, whose professional skill has been of benefit in every section of the book, our profound thanks are due: without her assistance the book would not have been possible. Alexander Shouvaloff and his staff at the Theatre Museum gave us free access to their holding and to materials not generally available, for which we are most grateful.

For the post-war period the theatre is fortunate in the number of skilled photographers who have worked to record its productions. We wish to express our thanks to the following who have given us permission to reproduce their work: Christopher Bailey, no. 177; Clive Barda, nos 225, 236, 237; Anthony Crickmay, nos 176, 187, 200, 226, 227, 228; Alan Cunliffe, no. 213; Frederika Davis, no. 193; Zoë Dominic, nos 163, 182, 203, 204, 214, 216, 232, 233; Edward Griffiths, no. 209; Angus McBean, no. 178; Edward Mandinian, nos 149, 161; Stuart Robinson, nos 205, 206, 212, 222; Houston Rogers, nos 166, 170, 177, 181, 189, 191, 202, 208; Roy Round, no. 183; Donald Southern, nos 190, 201, 217, 218, 220, 235, 238; Leslie E. Spatt, nos 196, 198, 207, 239; Michael Stannard, no. 197; Reg Wilson, nos 185, 195, 199, 210, 211, 215, 219, 221, 230, 231, 234.

We also wish to acknowledge the following agencies and institutions who have given permission for photographs to be reproduced: Keystone Press Agency, no. 192; *Sport & General*, no. 80; *The Times*, no. 167.

We wish to thank Diana Mitchell and Avril Jordan who have typed the text and captions of the book, and Philip de Bay who copied many of the photographs and prepared them for reproduction with considerable skill.

INTRODUCTION

THIS BOOK OUTLINES the story of the Royal Opera House, Covent Garden, from the opening of the first theatre on the present site in 1732 until the present day. It is concerned with not one but three theatres, each different in character and appearance; yet, despite the great fires of 1808 and 1856 which destroyed almost all traces of what had gone before, a sense of continuity has been preserved.

When John Rich opened the first Theatre Royal in Covent Garden in December 1732, it was an event of major importance. No new theatre of any substance had been opened in London since Vanbrugh's grandiose opera house in the Haymarket in 1705, while Rich's closest rival both geographically and commercially, the other Royal Patent theatre at Drury Lane, was an ageing structure designed in 1674 for the King's Men by Sir Christopher Wren. Rich's new building was made possible by the success of a single play at the small theatre he owned in Lincoln's Inn Fields. As Dr Johnson tells us, *The Beggar's Opera* 'was first offered to Cibber and his brethren at Drury Lane, and rejected; it then being carried to Rich, had the effect, as was ludicrously said, of making Gay *rich* and Rich *gay*.' But to pack a small theatre for a month with an unqualified success was a different prospect from filling a much larger house, week by week, season by season. From the outset, the management of Covent Garden, as we shall now refer to it, was faced with the economic nightmare of keeping their business solvent. In future decades many artistic ambitions were to be dashed by the fear of bankruptcy and the debtor's prison.

Covent Garden offered a fine building and, as the years passed, a great reputation and heritage, but to the man of business it seemed a Moloch demanding endless sacrifices to keep it in being. Rich tackled these problems with characteristic energy, and for almost thirty years contrived to present an astonishing variety of tragedies, comedies, farces, pantomines, concerts, ballets and operas. In truth, his technique was not to pioneer but to pluck other men's fruits. He lured Handel from the Haymarket and Arne from Drury Lane, while a procession of actors who quarrelled alternately with David Garrick at Drury Lane and John Rich at Covent Garden moved between the

two theatres. He created a fine troupe which included David Garrick, James Quin, Mrs Pritchard, Mrs Cibber and Peg Woffington, and presented many notable productions. Among these were several works by Handel—*Ariodante* and *Alcina* in 1735, *Acis and Galatea* and *Atalanta* in the following year and *Arminio, Berenice* and *Giustino* in 1737. The *Messiah* received its first London performance there in 1743. But above all, Rich sought to offer variety with a programme which in a single evening ranged from Shakespearean tragedy to burlesque, as the playbills of the day make plain. He knew the tastes and quality of his public.

The audience in the theatres of Georgian London is known to us through the images of Hogarth and Rowlandson. Garrick himself described it thus:

> Above t'was like Bedlam, all roaring
> And rattling. Below, the fine folk
> Were all curtsying and prattling.

Foreign visitors were amazed at the violence and rowdiness of the theatre audience which had more in common with the crowd at a Roman circus than the rapt playgoers of today. One visitor to Rich's Covent Garden wrote in his diary:

The uproar of the common people in the theatre before the curtain rises is simply frightful . . . [orange] peels being hurled on to the stage so that they lay in piles in front of the curtain. One spectator, unwisely staring up towards the tiers above felt 'a heap of orange peels, striking me with considerable force in the face'. . . . Another had his hat 'so saturated (I really do not know with what watery ingredients) that I was compelled to have it cleaned next day at the hatters'.

Yet despite this coarse and brutish behaviour, which was not, be it said, the exclusive preserve of the lower orders, Georgian theatregoers were both well-informed and critical. If they enjoyed the pantomime, in which Rich performed as Harlequin, and the light ballad operas like *The Beggar's Opera* or *Love in a Village* in which his son-in-law, the tenor John Beard, had the leading role, they also followed and appreciated more substantial works. The riot which took place in 1763 at a performance of Arne's *Artaxerxes* was directed at the supposedly rapacious management's increases in prices rather than at the quality of the production.

The formula which Rich established—the stock fare of the eighteenth-century stage—served his successors well. In 1782 and 1792 the theatre was remodelled, to give a greater capacity to the auditorium—the same commercial pressures lay behind Robert Adam's reconstruction of Drury Lane in 1775, and its subsequent enlargement by Henry Holland in 1794. Mrs Siddons called Covent Garden 'this vast wilderness' in contrast to the cramped intimacy of the earlier house. A new style of acting developed, as exemplified by

the Kemble family, more declamatory, yet more thrilling; productions likewise became florid and more costly. In September 1808, after a performance of *Pizarro*, the old theatre at Covent Garden burned to the ground. It was mourned by many but by none so eloquently as by John Philip Kemble who had since 1803 been part-owner and joint-manager of Covent Garden:

Yes, it has perished, that magnificent theatre, which for all the purposes of exhibition or comfort was the first in Europe. . . . Of all this . . . now remains but the Arms of England over the entrance of the theatre—and the Roman Eagle standing solitary in the Market Place.

Within nine days Kemble and his partner Harris were planning a new theatre; ten months later it was completed. The new building, designed in the neo-classical mode by Robert Smirke, was more in keeping with the spirit of the new age than the old had been. Natural catastrophe had the effect both in 1808 and later in 1856 of allowing the management of the theatre a *tabula rasa*, permitting them to build in accordance with their needs, rather than struggle within the confines of an antiquated shell. But grandeur had its price, and audiences were no more willing to pay for it than they had been in the days of Rich and John Beard. The prolonged 'Old Price' riots (illustrated in the body of this book) in the first days of the new theatre showed that although styles in drama had changed, the audience had not. Mrs Siddons, Kemble's sister, in Hazlitt's phrase 'Tragedy personified . . . the stateliest ornament of the public mind', still had to endure the insults which were commonplace half a century before. When she and her brother had been playing Coriolanus,

Mrs. Siddons was supplicating as Volumnia, the conqueror, her son, to spare his country; when every eye should have been riveted to the scene, every ear burning with the pure flame of patriot vehemence—at such a moment an apple was thrown upon the stage and fell between Mrs. Siddons and Mr. Kemble. . . . Kemble stepped forward and berated the audience, only to receive the shouted reply 'that this apple was thrown at some of the disorderly females in the boxes'.

It is easy to understand how the profitable mainstays of Covent Garden were pantomimes such as *Aladdin* (first performed in 1788), *Bluebeard*, and *Mother Goose* in which the great clown Grimaldi gave 92 consecutive performances when it was first presented in 1806. Equally popular were the 'spectaculars' as in 1811 with 'spahis and wild horses'. But the pattern of audiences was slowly altering, and the contrast between the audience seated in the stalls of Covent Garden in 1847 with those of three decades earlier is astonishing. Gone are Hogarthian derelicts, the apple throwers and the disorderly women; all are now prim and attentive. In the years of the Kembles' tenure of the theatre, and the brief interludes of Macready and

Madame Vestris, the foundations of later glories were laid.

From the beginning, Covent Garden had been a 'Theatre Royal', licensed by the Lord Chamberlain for all manner of theatrical performances. Nor was this an empty formula, since from 1662, only those theatres which possessed a Royal Patent were entitled to present plays to the public and charge for admission. Covent Garden and Drury Lane, the two 'Theatres Royal', fought constantly against interlopers, denouncing them to the authorities and enforcing court judgments against them. King George II had supported Handel's operas at Covent Garden, and his great-grandson, the future George IV, laid the foundation stone of the new theatre in 1808. (The stone is still visible to this day, in the Men's Chorus Washroom.) But only with the accession of Queen Victoria in 1837 did Royal Patronage acquire a more positive connotation. She had attended Covent Garden for the first time at the age of 14, and her comments in her Journal reveal much girlish enthusiasm: 'Pasta sang BEAUTIFULLY, Paganini played WONDERFULLY; Malibran, like Pasta, sang BEAUTIFULLY, with Taglioni dancing—likewise. Fanny Elssler also danced, VERY WELL.' With her marriage to her cousin, Prince Albert, a new and deeply musical influence entered the Royal family transmuting the Queen's native interest into a deeper and more practical knowledge. They became regular attenders at Covent Garden where the Queen liked the Royal Box and where, with the opening of the Royal Italian Opera in 1847, the performances were much to their taste. She acquired a certain discrimination; of the performance of *Robert le Diable* at Her Majesty's (the old King's Theatre in the Haymarket), she wrote: 'It is a most beautiful opera. The choruses were bad and the orchestra very often went wrong, but Jenny Lind was absolute perfection.' By contrast, she observed that at Covent Garden, 'The orchestra conducted by Costa was admirable.'

Royal support was both cause and effect of a profound change at Covent Garden. It made the theatre part of the social round of fashionable London, being used for state entertaining, as with the French Emperor, Napoleon III, and the German Emperor, Wilhelm II, and for other gala occasions of great splendour. The pantomimes and 'spectaculars' were as popular as ever, but in 1843, with the freeing of the theatres from many restrictions of the patent system, new and cheaper theatres sprang up with programmes better suited to baser tastes. In 1846, Covent Garden was reconstructed as an opera house, which opened in the following year as 'The Royal Italian Opera', thus turning away from its past.

In this new incarnation, Smirke's theatre had a brief existence. On 5 March 1856, after a Bal Masqué, the 'scene of undisguised indecency, drunkenness and vice', fire started inside the building. In the space of a few hours the theatre was utterly destroyed. The manager, Frederick Gye, who had sub-leased the theatre, hurried

home from Paris, and arrived in time to escort Queen Victoria around the ruins.

Yet, as almost half a century before, a new theatre was to rise phoenix-like from the ashes of the old. Gye set to work with demonic energy to raise the £70,000 needed to rebuild Covent Garden; almost all his assets had been destroyed in the fire. It is a measure of his success and of the confidence which he was able to inspire that he raised £120,000. He commissioned E. M. Barry, the son of the architect of the Houses of Parliament, to design his new opera house; the result was the building we know today, which was erected in a little over eight months. From the moment of its opening the opera house was recognised as an outstanding achievement. Barry had re-aligned the auditorium at right angles to that of the old theatre, so that it now lay on an east-west axis. The massive portico on Bow Street, designed to fulfil the ground landlord's (the Duke of Bedford) demand for 'grandeur', stood much higher than the earlier theatre; along its face were fixed the panels designed by Flaxman for the 1808 theatre, almost the only surviving relic of the earlier building. If Barry achieved stately ostentation outside, within the building the atmosphere was warm and welcoming, with one of the most beautiful auditoriums anywhere in the world. While the seating capacity was lower than in the earlier theatre, the comfort of the audience was immeasurably greater, and Barry crowned his success with the acoustic qualities which made Covent Garden renowned amongst opera houses.

From the opening of the new theatre on 15 May 1858, Covent Garden became dependent on a respectable, and often a society audience, less easily satisfied than earlier generations. Productions became more costly, and star performers were a *sine qua non*. Two singers, Adelina Patti and Nellie Melba, epitomised the grand style of the new opera house for more than sixty years. They performed to crowded houses, adored by their audiences; their sway over the managements of Covent Garden was absolute. They developed a great affection for Barry's new theatre—Melba once said that she thought of Covent Garden as home. In its new guise as an opera house Covent Garden needed more skilful management than before, balancing innovation with popular box office successes and striving always to present a season that would prove attractive to 'society'.

In the hands of two skilful and resourceful impresarios, Frederick Gye and Sir Augustus Harris, the theatre flourished; in the hands of lesser men, without the commercial acumen and strength to stand up to the demands made upon them by performers, it languished. Harris accomplished the marriage of wide artistic innovation with the support of fashionable London. In 1892 the theatre became the Royal Opera under his management, reflecting his success in expanding beyond the purely Italian repertory (or non-Italian works sung in Italian). In this he was aided by several eminent

figures, among them Lady de Grey (later Marchioness of Ripon) and Lady Charles Beresford. After his death in 1896, their dominance was formalised by the creation of the Grand Opera Syndicate which consisted of Lady de Grey's husband, her brother-in-law Harry Higgins, Lord Esher, George Faber (who owned the lease of the theatre) and Baron Frédéric d'Erlanger. Under their control, and with the close professional guidance of Neil Forsyth, secretary to the Syndicate (and both a connection by marriage and secretary to Sir Augustus Harris), together with the musical skill of Dr Hans Richter and Percy Pitt the 'musical adviser', a succession of great seasons were mounted before the First World War. Not only was their policy artistically successful, but also commercially prudent. Respectable profits were made year by year, and some £70,000, a remarkable sum for the times, was re-invested in the fabric of the theatre. A new stage was constructed—necessitating new scenery and new lighting—and electric light was installed throughout the building.

In the years of the Syndicate's operations more than forty new operas were presented, and great singers—such as Emmy Destinn, Enrico Caruso, Antonio Scotti and Giovanni Martinelli—appeared for the first time. In addition, the Russian ballet company created by Serge Diaghilev appeared in 1911 and made an immense stir, alerting England to developments which had already taken place in Europe. The subsequent flowering of ballet in Britain may have had its origin in those performances, which had been arranged by Sir Joseph Beecham, and were originally intended for Drury Lane until, on being offered a seat on the Grand Opera Syndicate, he changed theatres, bringing the ballet company with him.

During the First World War the Royal Opera House was used for occasional charity concerts but much of it became a furniture store. Meanwhile, in 1915 Sir Joseph's son Thomas, who had already appeared at Covent Garden conducting the 1910 winter and autumn seasons, formed his own company and gave several seasons of opera in English at various theatres including Drury Lane. Clearly the war impeded him but it is arguable that because of it the Beecham family was able to purchase the freehold of the Covent Garden estate; some years later it was acquired from them by a group headed by the financier Philip Hill who also bought the Beecham pharmaceutical business. Transfer of the freehold, however, did not affect the position of the Grand Opera Syndicate which continued to hold the lease of the Royal Opera House for a modest annual rental. Thomas Beecham was brought on to their board at the end of the war and shortly afterwards was appointed Artistic Director. He served in this capacity for one year but then negotiated a sub-lease from the Syndicate and was personally responsible for the 1920 season, presenting several operas in English in the winter and spring followed by a summer international season which included the return of Diaghilev's ballet company. His tenure of the opera house

was, however, short-lived because his finances were tangled and he had massive debts. He was finally declared bankrupt and for twelve years did not reappear at Covent Garden.

The next company to be heard at Covent Garden was the Carl Rosa, and it was as a member of that company that in the autumn of 1920 Eva Turner made her Royal Opera House debut. For the next twenty years she was to occupy a prominent place on the operatic scene, singing a wide range of parts both there and in many of the world's other leading opera houses. In 1921 the British National Opera Company was formed with Percy Pitt as its Musical and Artistic Director. It presented a short season of operas in English during the course of which Albert Coates conducted an English *Ring*; but because of the concentrated schedule and heavy demands upon the orchestra the general standard of performance left much to be desired.

The lease of the Royal Opera House was still held by the Grand Opera Syndicate which was revived in 1928 with a wealthy Hungarian financier, Mr F. A. Szarvasy, as Chairman. Colonel Eustace Blois was appointed Managing Director; he had no professional qualifications but was thought agreeable and musical. He was responsible for the engagement of Bruno Walter who came to Covent Garden to supervise regular annual seasons of German opera from 1924–31. At this time London was treated to many distinguished performances by, for instance, Lotte Lehmann, Elizabeth Schumann, Frida Leider, Lauritz Melchior, Friedrich Schorr and Richard Mayr. Bruno Walter himself conducted many of the operas of Wagner, Richard Strauss and Mozart, as well as Beethoven's *Fidelio*. The Italian repertory was not so well performed, though Tullio Serafin often conducted, Mariano Stabile was a notable Falstaff, and Beniamino Gigli made his debut in 1930, appearing regularly thereafter. It should, however, be remembered that these international seasons seldom lasted for more than two months.

In 1932 there was a short season of Grand Opera under Thomas Beecham but Szarvasy did not renew the lease and in December Covent Garden Properties, the company which owned the freehold and of which Philip Hill was Chairman, prepared plans to pull down the opera house and develop the site commercially. They were, however, persuaded to relent and even to make improvements. A new company, the Royal Opera House Company Limited, was then formed with Beecham in artistic charge and Geoffrey Toye as Managing Director in succession to Colonel Blois, who died in early 1933. Of the directors the most active was Lady Cunard, due to her particular friendship with Beecham.

Toye's relationship with Beecham was not good and he resigned in 1936. He was not replaced and Beecham was assisted on the management side by C. A. Barnard, and on the artistic side first

by Percy Heming, a baritone from Beecham's old company, and then in 1938 by Walter Legge, a brilliant planner of classical gramophone records and the founder of the Philharmonia Orchestra.

During the years leading up to the Second World War many fine performances were given and conductors included Wilhelm Furtwängler, Felix Weingartner and Vittorio Gui. There were also visits by Colonel de Basil's Ballets Russes, with Alexandra Danilova, Léonide Massine and David Lichine, and the so-called 'Baby Ballerinas' Irina Baronova, Tatiana Riabouchinska and Tamara Toumanova.

The outbreak of war brought all opera and ballet at Covent Garden to a halt but the theatre did not long remain silent, being leased by Mecca Cafés Ltd for use as a dance hall for the troops. As the war continued there was a serious risk that the theatre might not revert to its traditional role since Mecca Cafés had an option to renew their lease for five years from 1 January 1945 'unless the building was required for the presentation of opera and ballet'. In 1944 when the end of the war was in sight initiatives to save the theatre began. The prime movers were Lord Keynes (husband of the Russian ballerina Lydia Lopokova and Chairman of CEMA, the wartime Council for the Encouragement of Music and the Arts, later renamed the Arts Council of Great Britain), together with Leslie Boosey and Ralph Hawkes of the well-known music publishing firm.

Philip Hill prompted the impresario Harold Holt to approach Boosey and Hawkes who took their courage in both hands and, with an indication but no assurance that government support might be forthcoming, signed a lease of the theatre from 1 January 1945. They formed what was initially called an Advisory Council but later named the Covent Garden Committee, and subsequently the Covent Garden Trust. Lord Keynes was Chairman, and Kenneth Clark, Samuel Courtauld, William Walton, Professor E. J. Dent, Sir Stanley Marchant and Sir Steuart Wilson were members, as well, of course, as Leslie Boosey and Ralph Hawkes.

There were two immediate problems, first to obtain a definite promise of official financial support, and second to find someone to run the enterprise. The promise of support on a modest scale was obtained by Keynes, who was not only the Chairman of CEMA but was working at the heart of the Treasury and was deeply involved in post-war financial planning. For the position of General Administrator the choice fell upon David Webster, a Scotsman from Liverpool, who had held a senior post with a well-known department store but who during the war had been seconded to supervise munitions factories. He was an enthusiast for opera and ballet and Chairman of the Liverpool Philharmonic Society. Kenneth Clark had met and been impressed by him and recommended him to his colleagues. He was in fact already contracted to work for the Metal Box Company but was released from his contract and joined

Covent Garden in 1945, remaining until 1970, retiring at the age of 67.

It was rightly thought necessary to have security of tenure of the theatre and there was a suggestion that Covent Garden Properties might lease the building to another tenant. The Ministry of Works was therefore persuaded to exercise compulsory purchase powers, although in the event they only signed a forty-two-year lease at a relatively modest annual rental.

No significant headway could immediately be made in forming a national opera company but the Trust had the good fortune to have at hand a ready-made ballet company, provided that appropriate arrangements for its transfer could be made. Founded by Ninette de Valois with Frederick Ashton as choreographer and Constant Lambert as Musical Director the company had first appeared at Sadler's Wells Theatre in 1931. Through the years they had begun to develop a British style and approach to ballet. The directors at Sadler's Wells were reluctant to relinquish their prize but eventually agreed. Covent Garden acquired a bargain: sixteen ballets suitable for the Covent Garden stage, an accomplished group of dancers led by Margot Fonteyn and Robert Helpmann, and, most important of all, de Valois, Ashton and Lambert themselves. It was therefore possible to open the new Covent Garden with a gala performance of *The Sleeping Beauty*, designed by Oliver Messel with Margot Fonteyn and Robert Helpmann in the leading roles, on 20 February 1946, in the presence of the King and Queen and other members of the Royal Family. Throughout most of 1946 the Ballet Company had the theatre to itself except for a short season of Italian opera given by the San Carlo Company from Naples and a visit by Ballet Theatre from New York.

In spite of the fact that there was an opera company at Sadler's Wells containing several gifted singers who had done much valuable work, including the presentation of the world première of Benjamin Britten's *Peter Grimes*, it did not seem to the Trust to constitute a group upon which to rely for their projected National Opera Company. The Trust had clearly defined goals which were enunciated on the day that the appointment of Karl Rankl as Musical Director was announced. He had been a refugee from the Nazis, had served on the staff of many continental opera houses, including Vienna, Berlin and Prague, and represented a solid European tradition. He was prepared to work within these rules:

The principal singers will be chosen almost entirely from among those already known in this country, and from lesser-known singers discovered in auditions which are still being held in London and the Provinces. Nearly a thousand singers have been heard in these auditions. . . . The Trust believes that the development of opera in England, and indeed the formation of a style of performance, depends to a large extent on the use of the English Language. The performances of the resident company will therefore be given in English.

There can be little doubt that these self-imposed constraints made the task of the new company more difficult. There was, as Beecham had complained before the war, little native operatic tradition or a dedicated audience. In the post-war period, as indeed before, the stars were drawn for the most part from the international circuit, and it is a tribute to singers of the stature of Elizabeth Schwarzkopf, Kirsten Flagstad and Hans Hotter that they were willing to learn their roles in English. In December 1946 the first opera production, Purcell's *The Fairy Queen*, took place—a mixture of opera and ballet master-minded by Constant Lambert. In those first years, however, it was ballet which led the way. Most important was the boldness with which Ninette de Valois insisted upon bringing the principal classics into the repertoire, believing as she did that these must provide a solid base for the company's work. Her own ballets, especially *The Rake's Progress* and *Job*, were also well received. At the same time there were works which broke new ground, notably Frederick Ashton's *Symphonic Variations* (1946). The Ballet's visit to New York in 1949 was a triumph establishing the international standing of the company. Margot Fonteyn wrote of her first night in *The Sleeping Beauty* at the Met. in New York:

In the audience, applause greeted the Oliver Messel décor before anyone danced a step. When I ran out on to the stage there was a burst of sound. It drowned out the music and also some part of my mind, for I have never been able to remember anything between those first minutes of deafening applause on my entrance and the incredible reception after the third act pas de deux.

Feelings about the early productions of the opera company were mixed. Both Sadler's Wells and Glyndebourne presented opera, and critics were not slow to draw comparisons. Some productions, such as *Salome* in 1949 by Peter Brook, the new Director of Productions, had a hostile reception, but some of the criticism was perhaps self-interested, as in the case of Sir Thomas Beecham who attacked the Rankl regime as he was later to attack the next Musical Director, Rafael Kubelik, implying that he himself, rather than some 'foreigner', should be controlling the nation's operatic fortunes. Covent Garden's achievement was nevertheless to create a repertory of some thirty operas by the time Rankl's contract ended in 1951.

The position of Musical Director remained vacant for four years until the arrival of the Czech conductor, Rafael Kubelik, one of whose most notable achievements was the production of Berlioz's *The Trojans* in 1957. The opera was performed in English complete with both parts being given on the same evening, and it was an especial triumph for the Canadian tenor Jon Vickers, in the role of Aeneas.

A decade later Covent Garden could claim to be well on the way to its later triumphs. Erich Kleiber was the first of many

distinguished conductors who included Rudolf Kempe, Carlo Maria Giulini and Otto Klemperer, all of whom helped to give the orchestral playing a precision and authority it had sometimes lacked before. Kleiber had conducted the first performance of *Wozzeck* in Berlin in 1925 and now presented it at Covent Garden in January 1952, making something of a landmark in the history of the theatre.

There were also performances of works by British composers— Britten, Vaughan Williams, Bliss and Tippett—and a school of British conductors and singers was assuming a growing importance in the life of the opera house. This flowering of native talent began at a time when the principle of opera in English was slowly being disregarded. By this development Covent Garden became open to singers of the highest quality who were only prepared to sing in the languages in which they had prepared their roles. It soon also became clear that for British singers to achieve international reputations they too must know their parts in the original language. By the time that the opera company celebrated its tenth anniversary in 1956 much had already been achieved; it was capable of performing both the international repertoire and outstanding new British works. In 1971 Harold Rosenthal, writing in celebration of the twenty-five post-war years at Covent Garden said:

What is amazing is that in just a quarter of a century the Royal Opera has emerged as one of the leading operatic organisations in the world—and although obviously England has not achieved in twenty-five years what Italy and Germany did in some three hundred or so, the standards of the Royal Opera and the working atmosphere at Covent Garden are the envy of singers and conductors all over the world.

In the thirty-five years since the re-opening of Covent Garden there have been only two General Administrators, Sir David Webster and Sir John Tooley, three Chairmen of the Trustees/Board of Directors, Viscount Waverley, The Earl of Drogheda and Sir Claus Moser, and four Musical Directors, Karl Rankl (1946–51), Rafael Kubelik (1955–8), Sir Georg Solti (1961–71), immediately followed by Sir Colin Davis. During the two periods in which there was no Musical Director there were a number of important new productions. Notable among these were *Don Carlos* (1958) produced by Luchino Visconti and conducted by Carlo Maria Giulini, and *Lucia di Lammermoor* (1959) produced by Franco Zeffirelli and conducted by Tullio Serafin. Credit for the planning of these and other productions is to a large extent due to Lord Harewood who, having served for a short while on the Board of Directors, in 1953 joined the staff of the Royal Opera House where for seven years he played a significant role, serving in the capacity of Controller of Opera Planning (although the actual title was not conferred upon him by David Webster until a short while before he left Covent Garden to go to Edinburgh as Director of the Festival).

When Georg Solti became Musical Director in 1961 he brought in a very considerable spirit of initiative, above all demanding improved facilities for rehearsals and better working conditions. He was strongly conscious of the absence of Mozart's operas from the repertoire (other than *The Magic Flute*), an omission he quickly repaired. He was responsible for twenty-six new productions, with distinguished renderings of the works of Richard Strauss and Wagner, and a striking performance of Schoenberg's *Moses and Aaron*. During his tenure of office many eminent guest conductors came from abroad; in addition to British conductors who included Colin Davis, John Pritchard, Edward Downes, and Reginald Goodall, the public was able to hear many memorable performances by Otto Klemperer, Rudolf Kempe, Josef Krips, Carlo Maria Giulini, Claudio Abbado, and Pierre Boulez. During this time producers included Luchino Visconti for *Il Trovatore, La Traviata* and *Der Rosenkavalier*, and Franco Zeffirelli for those well known twins *Cavalleria Rusticana* and *Pagliacci*, and above all for his world-famous *Tosca* with Maria Callas and Tito Gobbi.

If the 1960s were a golden period for the opera, they were no less so for the ballet. It would be invidious to choose from amongst the many dancers of those days. Nevertheless we cannot fail to mention some choreographers and dancers—Frederick Ashton, Kenneth MacMillan and John Cranko, and George Balanchine and Jerome Robbins from America; Margot Fonteyn, Svetlana Beriosova, Nadia Nerina, Lynn Seymour, Merle Park, Michael Somes, David Blair and David Wall, and the memorable partnership of Antoinette Sibley and Anthony Dowell.

A distinctive feature of the post-war years has been the extent of which foreign companies have appeared at Covent Garden. The New York City Ballet and the Martha Graham Company have both appeared twice, and the Royal Danish Ballet, the American Ballet Theatre and Stuttgart Company once. Covent Garden also played host to the San Carlo Opera from Naples, the Bavarian State Opera from Munich, and the La Scala from Milan. Perhaps most significant for the British public were the succession of visits by the two leading ballet companies of the Soviet Union, the Bolshoi and the Kirov. It was during a visit to Paris in 1961 that Rudolf Nureyev defected from the latter company, and since then his appearances with the Royal Ballet, and above all his partnership with Margot Fonteyn, have become a legend. It would be hard to exaggerate the importance of his impact.

When Dame Ninette retired as Director in 1963 she handed over to Sir Frederick Ashton with whom she had been working for over thirty years. The already high standards continued to rise despite a strain imposed upon the company by regular touring, particularly in North America. Nor did Ashton's creative inspiration flag.

In 1970 Sir David Webster was succeeded by John Tooley who had been his deputy since 1955; Sir Frederick Ashton, while continuing to create ballets, in the same year handed over the Directorship of the Royal Ballet to Kenneth MacMillan (who was later succeeded by Norman Morrice). Sir Georg Solti retired in 1971 and was followed by Colin Davis; and in 1974 Lord Drogheda handed over to Sir Claus Moser as Chairman after serving for some sixteen years. The Board realised that they could not forever rely exclusively on subsidy from the Treasury through the Arts Council. Various schemes were adopted. The Friends of Covent Garden, primarily a supporting group, provided welcome financial assistance for a number of projects. The Society of the Royal Opera House pioneered a scheme to involve business in supporting the theatre and their direct heir, the Royal Opera House Trust, has been most successful in achieving substantial results. When the moment came to develop the fabric of the theatre following the removal of the flower, fruit and vegetable market, further money had to be raised and the Royal Opera House Development Appeal Fund came into existence. This too has met with a great measure of success.

It is difficult to treat history, let alone recent history, objectively, but it is beyond doubt that the thirty-five years since the last war have surpassed any period that has gone before. As we reach the end of this short account, the whole area around the theatre is in a fever of change. With the removal of the fruit and flower market the 'Piazza' has been restored to its earlier elegance, offering shops and restaurants, and creating an important tourist attraction. At the Royal Opera House itself many alterations and extensions are in hand, so that the theatre can look confidently ahead to the coming years, consolidating all that has been achieved since John Rich first came 'in his glory' to Covent Garden.

PART 1

Inspiration Breathes Life

ON EITHER SIDE of the stage of John Rich's new theatre in Covent Garden there stood the two Muses of Comedy and Tragedy. Above their heads ran a slogan which nightly proclaimed to the audience: 'Vivitur Ingenio', loosely translated 'Inspiration is the breath of life'. Rich was an inspired performer and manager and for many years greatly enhanced the theatrical life of London.

1 (PREVIOUS PAGE) THE OPENING of the
new theatre in Covent Garden in 1732,
in Hogarth's sardonic portrayal of
Rich's Glory:

Not with more glory through the Streets of Rome,
Return'd great Conqueror in Triumph home
Than, proudly drawn with Beauty at his side
We see gay R*** in gilded Chariot ride.

2 JOHN RICH (*c.* 1692–1761)

The son of Christopher Rich, described by a contemporary
dramatist as 'an old snarling lawyer, a waspish ignorant
pettifogger', he inherited from his father a fascination for the
world of the theatre, and, more significant, a share in the Royal
Patent granted by King Charles II to permit stage performances.
After his father's death in 1714 he took over the management of
the small theatre in Lincoln's Inn Fields. The enormous success of
The Beggar's Opera, which brought him over £11,000 in takings,
allowed him to develop a plan for a much larger theatre. In
1726, two years before *The Beggar's Opera* was presented, he had
begun to obtain leases in the area of Covent Garden, and in 1731,
he completed the process after complicated negotiations with the
ground landlord, the Duke of Bedford. Building began in April
1731, and after many disputes and wrangles with architect and
builders, it was completed by November 1732. Rich's career at
Covent Garden began with the first performance in December
1732 and lasted until his death

3 *The Beggar's Opera*, the play which enabled John Rich to build his grand new theatre in Covent Garden

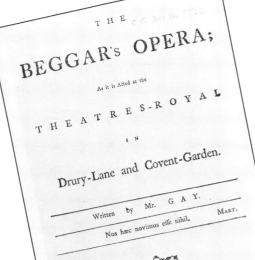

4 THE ENTRANCE to Rich's theatre in Covent Garden, in the arcade of the Covent Garden piazza, 1791

5 JOHN RICH as Harlequin

Rich was a notable mime, and his Harlequin, which he performed under the stage name of Lun, after the great Parisian Harlequin, was the basis of the English tradition of pantomime as later performed at Covent Garden. He was an entirely natural performer on stage, and a likeable character off stage, with a penchant for cats and beautiful women: Pope once wrote:

Ye Gods! Shall Cibber's son without rebuke
Swear like a Lord, *or Rich outwhore a Duke.*

He also enjoyed the company of men, and helped to found 'The Sublime Society of the Beefsteaks' in 1735

6 GEORGE FREDERICK HANDEL (1685–1759)
Despite Handel's eminence as a composer, his operas and
oratorios were not a financial success. Attendances at some of his
performances were increased by the device of combining a Handel
work with a performance by the leading dancer, Madame Sallé.
Handel produced six new operas, two pasticcios, a secular choral
work, and a new oratorio at Covent Garden in the years 1734–7:
the privilege cost him over £10,000, and his health was ruined
through overwork

7 A CONCERT in the first theatre at Covent Garden. This is the theatre built by John Rich, but altered internally in
1782 and 1792 to increase the seating capacity. Handel's famous organ can be seen in the centre of the stage, and the
candelabra on the tiers, which were the means of lighting the theatre. By the nature of the audience, the production is
clearly an oratorio rather than a more popular production: the contrast with some of the other audience pictures by
Rowlandson is marked

8 THOMAS ARNE (1710–78)

Now best remembered as the composer of *Rule Britannia*, Arne, who came to Covent Garden from Drury Lane in 1760, was responsible for some of the early operas, other than those by Handel (and Gay's perennially successful *Beggar's Opera*) which appeared at the theatre. His *Love in a Village* provided a fine role for his friend, John Beard, who had taken over the management of the theatre after Rich's death, and his adaptation of the Italian libretto by Metastasio, together with his own music, in *Artaxerxes*, achieved considerable success. It was unfortunate, however, that a performance of *Artaxerxes* was chosen as the occasion for a mob of ruffians led by a 'gentleman of independent fortune', one Thaddeus Fitzpatrick, to cause an uproar in protest at the management's decision to abolish reduced prices for the second half of the performance, as was the custom in the London theatres of the day

9 THE INTERIOR of Rich's theatre at Covent Garden, 1763. The entrance doors at the side of the stage can be seen, and the actors playing forward on the stage as was the custom of the time. Not visible are the two armed guardsmen, who were required to stand on stage throughout each performance, with musket and bayonet, for fear of riot or other disturbance. In one production at Covent Garden at the time of the Jacobite Rising of 1745, Peg Woffington, 'dressed in the new Blue uniform, with Firelock (and fixed Bayonet) in her hand' was intended to go up and shake hands 'with one of the Stage Grenadiers'. However, given the frequent disturbances in the London theatres, the soldiers seem to have been singularly ineffective in overawing the tumultuous mob on this occasion – they invaded the stage during a performance of Arne's *Artaxerxes*

10 JOHN BEARD (*c.* 1717–91) in Arne's opera *Love in a Village*, 1767

The leading English tenor of his day, he began his career in the Chapel Royal, and on the operatic stage in the Handel seasons at Covent Garden. He appeared regularly in lighter roles at Drury Lane, and married the daughter of the Earl of Waldegrave, who died in 1753. In 1759, he remarried, his second wife being the daughter of John Rich, the proprietor of Covent Garden, and he returned to Rich's company. After the death of his father-in-law in 1761, Beard took over the management of the company, but he was becoming increasingly deaf. In 1767 he took his leave of the public in a final performance of *Love in a Village*, his favourite role

11 PEG WOFFINGTON (*c.* 1718–60)

The 'gay, affable, obliging good-natured Woffington' was unique among all the great actresses who appeared at Covent Garden, not only for her talents, but for her loyalty. Her whole career, apart from her early years in Dublin, was spent at Covent Garden, from her first performance as Sylvia in *The Recruiting Officer* in 1740, until her final performance some seventeen years later, when she broke down on stage

12 SPRANGER BARRY (1719–77) and his wife, ANN DANCER (1734–1801)

One of the few actors thought able to rival David Garrick, Barry left Drury Lane to shine more brightly in the Covent Garden company. But he found an equally quarrelsome troupe, and after five seasons, with some memorable performances, he departed to his native Dublin, declaring that without him Rich's empire would collapse. . . .

13 MARIE SALLÉ (1707–56)
The great rival of Camargo, she
appeared regularly at Covent Garden,
dancing during many of Handel's
operas. She was a noted beauty, with
both Pope and Gay elaborating on her
charms

14 SATIRE on the Youthful Prodigy, Master Betty, 1804

15 MASTER BETTY, the Young Roscius, in the Character of Douglas, 1805

William Henry West Betty (1791–1874) had a theatrical career which lasted little more than a year. The infant prodigy was called 'the Young Roscius' (Quintus Roscius being the most famous Roman actor) in conscious imitation of David Garrick, who was known as the English Roscius. Cartoonists lampooned the mania which gripped the public. He caught the fancy of a romantic audience, inspired by his beauty and innocence. But the 'Theatrical BUBBLE', as Gillray described it, could not last, and once the novelty had become stale, Betty's triumph was ended

16 R. B. SHERIDAN (1751–1816) presents the Infant Prodigy, Master Betty, to Royalty, 1804. It was proposed that the House of Commons should suspend its sitting so that members should be able to see the young Wonder of the Theatrical World

Theatre Royal, Covent-Garden.

This present MONDAY, Sept. 19, 1808,

Will be acted the Play of

PIZARRO.

The Musick composed by Mr. KELLY.

PERUVIANS.

Ataliba by Mr. MURRAY, Rolla by Mr. KEMBLE, Fernando by Miss PRICE,
Orozembo, Mr CHAPMAN, Huaipa by Mr. BLANCHARD
Topac by Miss M. Bristow, Huscah by Mr. Jefferies,
Orano, Mr. THOMPSON, Harin, Mr. LOUIS, Capal, Mr SARJANT, Rima Mr WILDE,
Cora by Mrs. H. JOHNSTON,
(Being her first appearance in that character.)
Zuluga by Mrs BOLOGNA.
Priests, Virgins, Matrons, in the

TEMPLE OF THE SUN.

High Priest by Mr. BELLAMY,
Mess. T. Blanchard, Burden, Denman, Everard, Fairclough, King, Lambert, Lee, Linton, Odwell
Smalley, Street, Taylor, Terry, Tett, Treby, Williams—Mesdames Benson, L. Bologna, Bolton
Bristow, Cox, Cranfield, De Camp, Fawcett, Findlay, Follett, Grimaldi, Hagemann, Iliff, Leserve
Liston, Martyr, Masters, Meadows, Price, Ridgway, Watts, Whitmore.

SPANIARDS.

Pizarro by Mr. POPE, Alonzo by Mr. C. KEMBLE, Las Casas by Mr. CRESWELL,
Almagro by Mr. DAVENPORT, Davila by Mr MENAGE, Gonzalo by Mr. ATKINS
Valverde by Mr. CLAREMONT, Gomez by Mr. FIELD, Pedro, Mr HOLLAND,
Sancho Mr Brown, Bernal Mr Powers, Pablo Mr W. Murray, Sentinel Mr. EMERY.
Elvira by Mrs. SIDDONS.

To which will be added, *(4th time)* the last new Farce called The

Portrait of Cervantes;
Or, The PLOTTING LOVERS.

Murillo by Mr. MUNDEN,
Don Carlos Merida by Mr. JONES,
Don Guzman by Mr. BRUNTON, Scipio by Mr. BLANCHARD,
Sancho by Mr. LISTON, Father Benito by Mr. WADDY,
Alguazils, Mess. Holland, Brown, Grant, Heath, Sarjant.
Lucetta by Mrs. GIBBS,
Isabella by Miss BRISTOW.

Printed by R. Macleish, 2, Bow-street.   Vivant Rex & Regina.

On Wednesday, the Comick Opera of
The ENGLISH FLEET in 1342.
Count de Mountfort, Mr. TAYLOR, Capt. Fitzwater, Mr. INCLEDON,
Philip, Mr. BLANCHARD, Valentine, Mr. BELLAMY, Mainmast, Mr. MUNDEN,
Katharine, Mrs. DICKONS, Isabel, Miss BOLTON.
To which will be added the Grand Serious Panto
RAYMOND AND AGNES; or, The BLEE
On Friday, Shak historical
KING
Quee
To which
On account of the

17 JOHN BULL displays his contempt or boredom at the Italian style of opera. One diarist summed up the British attitude to the offerings:

I can't say I was greatly entertained, tho' the music was very pleasing. There is something very absurd and truly characteristic of the present Age in supporting a set of people at immense expense to perform plays in a language which very few understand.

18 IT WAS after this performance of *Pizarro* that the theatre caught fire and was burned to the ground

PART 2

The Phoenix

FIRE TWICE RAZED the theatre to the ground and twice a new building emerged from the ashes. In each case the tradition of the theatre was transformed, shaking off those parts of its heritage found to be irrelevant. The second theatre was the stage of the Kembles and Edmund Kean and the third became a great international opera house.

19 (SEE PREVIOUS PAGE) DESCRIPTION of the second theatre at Covent Garden:
The chief entrance to the Boxes is under the Portico in Bow-street. On the left of
the *vestibule* is the grand stair-case, which leads to the ante-room, in which is a fine
figure of Shakespeare. From the ante-room you come into the lobby of the lower
tier of boxes; which is the Ionic style of architecture, and is divided with arched
recesses, the semi-circular parts of which are filled with paintings from various
scenes of Shakespeare painted in *relief*. The fronts of the boxes are elegant,
though simple; a gold fretted flower, of antique form, runs along each tier, upon
a pale coloured ground: above and below the flowers are rows of stars. None of
the boxes project beyond the others, in the manner of those usually termed stage-
boxes; and the fronts are perpendicular, without any of that rotundity which
rather hurt than enrich the *coup d'oeil* in the former theatre. Slender pillars, richly
gilt, separate the boxes; and from a golden bracket, above each pillar, is
suspended a chandelier of cut glass: these chandeliers are novel in their form.
The seats of the boxes are covered with light blue cloth, and the seats are more in
number than in the boxes of the former theatre. The pit is divided by two
passages through the middle of it, and the seats are much elevated above each
other. The two-shilling gallery is more ample than has been represented, and the
slips are very wide and commodious. The most remarkable novelty consists in
the construction of the shilling gallery: here the architect, to preserve the
uniformity of his design, has rested the piers of a row of arches which support
the roof, in such a manner that the gallery is divided into five parts, resembling
separate boxes.

20 IMPRESSION of the theatre built by Smirke, as seen in Rowlandson's
Dr. Syntax, during a performance of Shakespeare's *Henry IV Part 1*.
Syntax's comments were distinctly critical:

It is not good, this vast profound:
I see no well-wrought columns here!
No attic ornaments appear;
Nought but a washy wanton waste
Of gaudy tints and puny taste
Too large to hear—too long to see
Full of unmeaning symmetry.

21 THE PLAYBILL announcing the opening production at the new theatre which
opened at Covent Garden on Monday 18 September 1809

The Publick are respectfully informed that the

New Theatre Royal, Covent-Garden,
WILL BE OPENED
This present MONDAY, Sept. 18, 1809,
With the Tragedy of

MACBETH.

With entirely new Scenery, Dresses, & Decorations.
The Overture and Symphonies between the Acts by Mr. WARE.
The Vocal Music by MATTHEW LOCK.
Duncan, King of Scotland, by Mr. CHAPMAN,
Malcolm by Mr. CLAREMONT, Donalbain by Mr. MENAGE,
Macbeth by Mr. KEMBLE, Macduff by Mr. C. KEMBLE,
Banquo by Mr. MURRAY, Fleance by M. BRISTOW,
Lenox by Mr. CRESWELL, Rosse by Mr. BRUNTON,
Siward Mr ATKINS, Seyton Mr JEFFERIES, Physician Mr DAVENPORT
Officers, Mess. Thompson & Wilde, Chamberlains, Mess. Heath & Truman
Gentlemen, Mess. Brown, Grant, Holland, Louis, Powers, Sarjant,
Lady Macbeth by Mrs. SIDDONS,
Gentlewoman by Mrs HUMPHRIES,
Ladies Mesdames Bologna, I. Bologna, Cox, Cranfield Follett, Whitmore.
Apparitions, Mr. Field, Miss S. Goodwin, Miss C. Goodwin,
Hecat by Mr BELLAMY, Witches, Mess. BLANCHARD, FARLEY, SIMMONS

To which will be added the musical Entertainment of

The QUAKER.

Steady by Mr. INCLEDON, Easy by Mr. DAVENPORT,
Lubin by Mr. TAYLOR, Solomon by Mr. LISTON,
John by Mr HOLLAND, Thomas by Mr. TRUMAN,
Gilli Miss BOLTON, Cecily Miss LESERVE, Floretta Mrs LISTON.
Before the Play, an Occasional Address on the opening of the Theatre,
Will be spoken by Mr. KEMBLE.
Places for the Boxes to be taken of Mr. BRANDON, at the Box-office in Hart-street.
The Doors will be opened at HALF past FIVE, and the Play begin at HALF past SIX.

THE PROPRIETORS, having completed the NEW THEATRE within the
time originally promised, beg leave respectfully to state to the Publick the absolute
necessity that compels them to make the following advance on the prices of admission:
FIRST PRICE.   HALF PRICE.
BOXES, Seven Shillings. ——— Three Shillings and Sixpence.
PIT.   Four Shillings. ——— Two Shillings, as usual.
The LOWER and UPPER GALLERIES will remain at the old Prices.
On the late calamitous destruction of their property, the Proprietors, encouraged
by the remembrance of former patronage, instantly and cheerfully applied themselves
to the erection of a new Theatre, defigning only, as it, without enlarging the audience-
part of the edifice, it might afford the Publick improved accommodation, and security,
and at the same time present an additional ornament to the Metropolis of the British
Empire This, their most anxious wish, they flatter themselves, they have solidly
effected, not only within the short space of ten months from the laying of the foundations, but under the enormously expensive disadvantage of circumstances singularly
unfavourable to building.—When it is known that no less a sum than one hundred
and fifty thousand pounds has been expended in order to render this Theatre worthy
of British Spectators, and of the Genius of their native Poets:—when, in this under-
taking, the inevitable accumulation of, at least, a sixfold rentage is positively stated to
be incurred;—and when, in addition to these pressing incumbrances, the encreased
and rapidly encreasing prices of every article indispensable to dramatick representations
come to be considered—the Proprietors persuade themselves that in their proposed regu-
lation they shall be honoured with the concurrence of an enlightened & liberal Publick.

The attention of the Publick is requested to the following description of the

Entrances to the new Theatre.

BOXES.
The principal Entrance is at the Portico in Bow-street, leading to the stone Hall
and Staircase.
The West Entrance is in Prince's-Place, leading from the Piazza in Covent-
Garden to the stone Staircase and Ante-room.

PIT.
The principal Entrance is from the Piazza, through Bedford-Avenue, leading by
five doors to the stone Vestibule and Staircases.
The East Entrance is in the Arcade, South of the Portico in Bow-Street, leading
to the same Vestibule and Staircases.

LOWER GALLERY.
The principal Entrance is from the Piazza, through Bedford-Avenue.

LOWER and UPPER GALLERIES.
The Entrance is at the Eastern extremity of Bedford-Avenue in Bow-Street.

ANNUAL BOXES.
The Entrances are in Prince's-Place, leading from Hart-Street;—and in the
Arcade, North of the Portico in Bow-Street.

⁎⁎ Ladies and Gentlemen going to the Theatre by any of the Entrances in Bow-
Street, are requested to order their Coachmen to set down with their horses heads
towards Long-Acre,—and to drive off through Little Bow-Street.
Ladies and Gentlemen coming to the Annual Boxes in Prince's-Place, are requested to order their Coachmen to drive to the Theatre through Long-Acre and
down James-Street into Hart-Street,—or through Covent-Garden up James-Street
into Hart-Street,—and to drive from the Theatre through the same Streets.

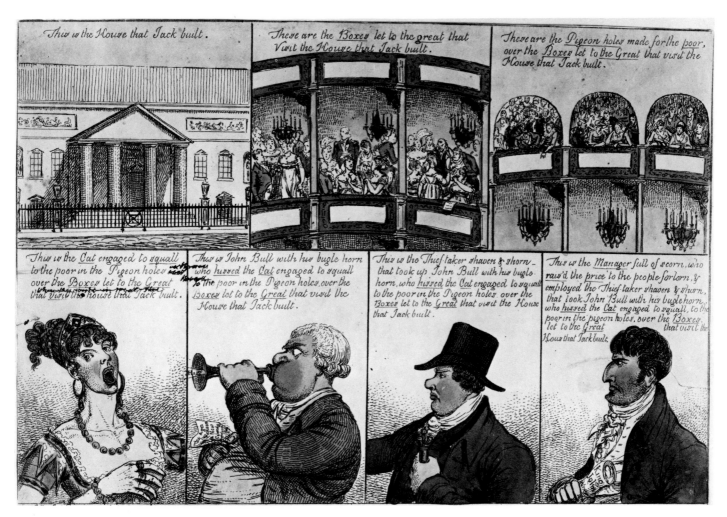

22 THE HOUSE THAT JACK BUILT. *Jack* was John Kemble, who built the new theatre, and increased the seat prices. The Cat is *Madame Catalani*, the highly paid soprano, whom patriotic *John Bull* believed was paid so much to squall her *foreign* rubbish that Englishmen were forced to pay more to go to the theatre. The *Thief Taker* was engaged to restore order in the theatre. Medals were struck, slogans and broadsheets filled the streets around the theatre, and eventually the management was forced to climb down

23 IN 1809, John Kemble attempted to recoup some of the heavy costs of rebuilding the theatre which burned down in 1808 by increasing seat prices. The consequence was a series of riots known as the OP (Old Price) riots. The management responded to the unrest by hiring thugs and prizefighters to eject the rioters, and the Riot Act was read by magistrates from the stage. Rowlandson has caught both the turbulence of the times, with men armed with clubs and the bandaged rioter in the lower boxes, and the wide social mixture of the audience, from the prim miss being poked with an umbrella to the pock-marked inebriate vomiting from the upper tier. Nor has he forgotten to put the pigeons in their 'pigeon holes'!

24 THE CHEAPEST GALLERY seats, sold at one shilling, were abolished by the Covent Garden management, and 'cooped' up the gallery audience in 'pigeon holes' at the top of the theatre, 1809. Rowlandson's drawing, published in February 1811, gives a fair impression of the character and behaviour of the popular audience in Georgian England. The 'pigeon holes' were finally removed in 1812, as a result of vociferous public complaints

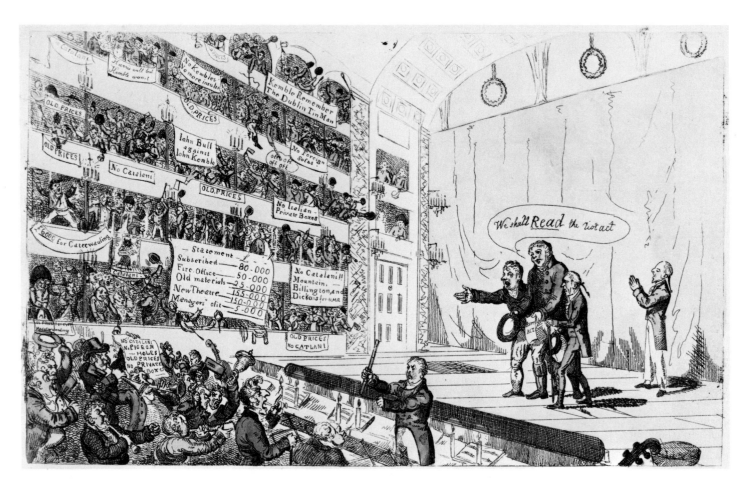

25 THE MAGISTRATES reading the Riot Act upon the stage at Covent Garden in the midst of the Old Price riots. The placards hanging from the tiers give a fair impression of the rioters' grievances. 1809

26 THE UNDISPUTED KING OF CLOWNS, JOSEPH GRIMALDI (1778–1837)

The son of the ballet master at Drury Lane, Grimaldi first appeared on stage at the age of 3; his first appearance at Covent Garden had to wait until 1806, when he delighted audiences as Harlequin in *Harlequin and Mother Goose*, written for him by Thomas Dibdin. For the next seventeen years he was the key to the fortunes of Covent Garden, for a Grimaldi performance meant the certainty of a full house. He was a pioneer of remarkable talent, advancing clowning from mere horseplay and buffoonery into a highly specialised branch of acting. Even in retirement, he was much fêted and respected, and the warmth and depth of his character is revealed in his *Memoirs* edited by Charles Dickens

27–32 A Tribe of Kembles

From 1803, when John Philip Kemble and his sister Sarah Siddons bought an interest in Covent Garden, the fortunes of the theatre were tied to the extraordinary talents of the Kemble family. Together with their brothers, Charles and Stephen, and their nieces, Frances (Fanny) and Adelaide, the appearances of the members of the Kemble family on the stage of Covent Garden spanned almost forty years.

As actors, John Philip and Sarah Siddons were beyond compare, and as a manager of Covent Garden J. P. Kemble was effective and far-sighted. He organised the rebuilding of the theatre after the fire of 1808, weathered the obloquy of the Old Price riots, and retired, universally respected, in 1817. His brothers proved less adept as managers, and Covent Garden sank under the vagaries of the younger Kembles and a procession of others eager to prove that they could make a success of the theatre

27 JOHN PHILIP KEMBLE (1757–1823)

28 CHARLES KEMBLE (1775–1854)

M.ᴿ STEPH.ⁿ KEMBLE,
AS
FALSTAFF.

29 STEPHEN KEMBLE (1758–1822)

Mrs. Siddons
(For this Night only.)

For the Benefit of
MR. and MRS. C. KEMBLE.

THEATRE ROYAL, COVENT-GARDEN

This present WEDNESDAY, June 9, 1819,
Will be acted the Tragedy of

DOUGLAS.

Norval by Mr. C. KEMBLE,
Lord Randolph by Mr. EGERTON,
Glenalvon by Mr. MACREADY,
The Stranger by Mr. YOUNG,
Donald by Mr CLAREMONT,
Lady Randolph *(for this night only)* by Mrs SIDDONS,
Anna by Miss FOOTE.

After which, (by particular defire) an Interlude called

PERSONATION.

Lord Henry, Mr. ABBOTT, Lady Julia, Mrs. C. KEMBLE.
To which will be added a Farce, called

THE CRITICK:
Or, A TRAGEDY REHEARSED.

Sir Fretful Plagiary, Mr. W. FARREN, Puff, Mr. JONES,
Dangle, Mr CONNOR, Sneer, Mr EGERTON, Under Prompter, Mr King,
Mrs Dangle, Miss LOGAN.
Tragedians.
Lord Burleigh, Mr Williams, Governor, Mr Comer, Earl of Leicefter, Mr Jefferies
Sir Walter Raleigh, Mr Treby, Sir Christopher Hatton, Mr. Simmons
Master of the Horse, Mr ATKINS, Beef Eater, Mr. J. RUSSELL,
Don Ferolo Whiskerandos, Mr. LISTON,
Sentinels, Meff. Heath & Grant, Nieces, Mefdames Coates and Sexton,
Tilburina, Mrs. GIBBS. To conclude with a Grand

Sea Fight, & the Destruction of the Spanish Armada,

For the accommodation of a number of Ladies and Gentlemen who have not
been able to procure Places in the Boxes, the Orchestra will, for this evening,
be occupied by a part of the audience, and the Symphonies between the Acts
be played behind the Scenes.

Tickets for the Orchestra will be admitted at the Private Box Door, Bow-street
VIVAT REX.

Cozening; or, Half an Hour in France,
continues to be most enthusiastically received—The correct Personation of the various
Characters by Mr. YATES, was universally acknowledged by the acclamations of
the audience—It will be repeated every evening—Benefits excepted.

Tomorrow, for the Benefit of Miss STEPHENS (by Special Order) and last time this Season,
the Opera of The MARRIAGE of FIGARO.
Count Almaviva, Mr. JONES, Fiorello, Mr. DURUSET,
Figaro by Mr. LISTON, Antonio (the Gardener) Mr. FAWCETT,
Countess Almaviva by Mrs. DICKONS, Susanna by Miss STEPHENS.
With an Interlude called SYLVESTER DAGGERWOOD.
And the Operatick Drama of The LIBERTINE. Zerlina, Miss STEPHENS.
On Friday, for the Benefit of Mr EMERY, the Opera of ROB ROY MACGREGOR.
Rob Roy (first time) Mr. EMERY, Diana Vernon, Miss STEPHENS.
With the Farce of X. Y. Z.
On Saturday, (16th time) the new musical Drama of The HEART of MID-LOTHIAN.
With COZENING—And (29th time) the Farce of A ROLAND for an OLIVER.
On Monday, 2d time, Shakspeare's Tragedy of JULIUS CÆSAR.
With the revived Pantomime of MOTHER GOOSE.
On Tuesday, for the Benefit of Mr. LISTON, the Comedy of The RIVALS.
With (by permission of the Proprietor of the Surrey Theatre) DON GIOVANNI.

30 POSTER advertising *Douglas*, with
Sarah Siddons as Lady Randolph,
9 June 1819

31 SARAH SIDDONS (1755–1831)

32 A HANDBILL announcing John Philip Kemble's final
performance in the theatre, 23 June 1817

He was much insulted when the audience showed a marked
preference for the act of an Italian rope-walker which followed his
performance as Sir Giles Overreach. However, on this his final
appearance, as Coriolanus, Hazlitt says, 'He played the part as well
as he ever did, with as much freshness and vigour. . . . His look,
his action, his expression of the character were the same as they
ever were; they could not be finer.'

33 THE FAREWELL dinner for J. P. Kemble, 27 June 1817

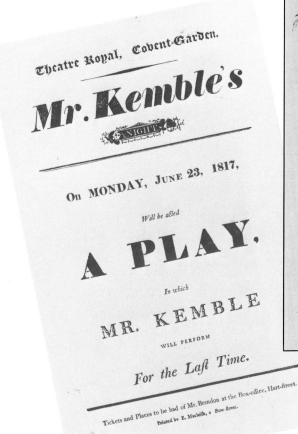

34 EDMUND KEAN (*c.* 1787–1833) as Othello

On 25 March 1833, Kean played Othello, with for the first time
his son Charles as Iago. He drew Charles to the footlights and
presented his heir to the audience, to a storm of cheering. He
began the performance conscious of a great sense of weakness; he
told Charles before the third act: 'Mind that you keep before me
. . . I don't know if I shall be able to kneel but if I do be sure that
you lift me up.' Before the climax of the play was reached, Kean
collapsed, throwing out his arms to his son saying, 'O God, I am
dying. . . . Speak to them for me.' So ended the career of perhaps
the most remarkable of English actors, of whom Coleridge was
reputed to have said that his acting 'was like reading Shakespeare
by flashes of lightning'

THEATRE ROYAL, COVENT GARDEN.

The Public is respectfully informed, that

Mr. KEAN

was last Thursday received in the character of **SHYLOCK** with acclamations;—and in order to meet the generally expressed desire that he should appear with his Son,

The Tragedy of OTHELLO

will be acted this evening,

when they will perform together, for the first time.

This present MONDAY, March 25, 1833, Shakspeare's Tragedy of

OTHELLO.

The Duke of Venice, Mr. RANSFORD,

Brabantio, Mr. DIDDEAR,   Gratiano, Mr. TURNOUR,

Lodovico, Mr. PAYNE,   Montano, Mr. HAINES,

Othello   by   Mr.   KEAN,

Cassio,   Mr. ABBOTT,

Iago, *(first time)*   Mr.   CHARLES KEAN,

Roderigo, Mr. FORESTER,   Antonio, Mr. IRWIN,   Julio, Mr. T. Matthews

Giovanni, Mr. J. COOPER,   Luca, Mr. BRADY,   Lorenzo Mr. Bender

Messenger Mr MEARS, Marco Mr Collet, Cosmo Mr Heath, Paolo Mr Stanley

Desdemona, *(first time)*   Miss   E. TREE,

Emilia, Mrs. LOVELL.

After which, (3d time) A NEW FARCE, in Two Acts. called

A Nabob for an Hour

Mr. Frampton, Mr. ABBOTT,   Sam Hobbs, Mr. BARTLEY,

Dick Dumpy, Mr. KEELEY,

Emma Leslie, Miss SYDNEY,   Nanny Scraggs, Mrs. KEELEY.

To conclude with the Grand Ballet of

MASANIELLO.

Masaniello, *(Fisherman of Portici)* Mons. COULON,

Alphonse, *(Viceroy of Naples)* Mons. THEODORE GUERINOT,

Pietro, Mr. PAYNE, Borella, Mr. GOURIET, Morino, Mr. MICHAU, Lasarini, Mr. T. MATTHEWS

Francisco, Mr. CHICKINI, Lazzaroni, Mr. ELLER, Lorenzo, Mr. IRWIN, Selva, Mr. BERTRAM

Fenella, *(Sister of Masaniello)* Madame PROCHE GIUBILEI.

Elvire, *(Wife of Alphonse)* Mlle. ADELE,   Dame of Honour, Miss THORPE.

On this occasion, the Vocal Parts will be sustained by

Mess. WILSON, I. BENNETT, DURUSET, HENRY, MORLEY. G. PENSON, RANSFORD, STANSBURY

Mesdames H. CAWSE DALY. HORTON, INVERARITY, KEELEY, LEE, E. ROMER, SHIRREFF.

In Act I. A PAS DEUX by Mons. THEODORE GUERINOT and Mlle. ADELE.

In act II.   A BOLERO by MONS. COULON & MADAME PROCHE GIUBILEI.

A TARENTELLE by Mr. MICHAU and Mrs. VEDY.

PLACES for the BOXES to be had of Mr. NOTTER, at the Box-Office, Hart-Street, from Ten till Four.

Auber's new Opera of

THE COINERS,

Or, The SOLDIER's OATH,

having been honoured with the most COMPLETE SUCCESS,

and announced for repetition amidst general and enthusiastic

applause, will be performed To-morrow & Saturday next,

And Three Times a Week after Easter.

A NABOB FOR AN HOUR

having again been received with roars of laughter and applause, will be repeated

Every Evening until further notice.

Tomorrow, (2d time) AUBER's New Opera of **The COINERS**, or the Seldier's Oath

With (4th time) **A Nabob for an Hour.**

To conclude with (38th time) the new Drama of **NELL GWYNNE.**

On Wednesday, **(Last Night but One)** the highly popular New Dramatic Oratorio, called

The Israelites in Egypt; or, the Passage of the Red Sea.

On Easter-Monday will be produced a New **SERIO-COMIC LEGENDARY FAIRY TALE.**

(which has been long in preparation,) to be called

The ELFIN SPRITE,

AND

The Grim Grey Woman.

With new Scenery, Machinery, Dresses, and Decorations.

The principal Characters by Mr. KEELEY, Mr. W. H. PAYNE, Mr. HAINES, Mr. HENRY,

Mr. F. MATTHEWS, Mrs. VINING, Miss ROMER, Miss POOLE, Mrs. KEELEY.

Printed by W. REYNOLDS, 9. Exeter-street, Strand.

35 Playbill announcing the performance of Othello in which Kean appeared for the first time with his son, Charles

36 CARL MARIA VON WEBER (1786–1826), conducting *Der Freischütz* at
Covent Garden

Weber came to London in March 1826 to take up the post of musical director at
Covent Garden, and from his first appearance his success was ensured:

As I stepped to the front of the box to have a look round, someone in the
audience shouted 'Weber! Weber is here!' and at once I drew quickly back, but
such a shouting, clapping and cries of 'Viva' broke out, that there was no end to
it until I had made several more appearances.

When his new opera *Oberon*, with a libretto by Planché, was first performed on
12 April 1826, new heights were reached. Weber wrote to his wife: 'I have this
evening had such a complete success as perhaps never before. The thrill and
emotion of such a complete and unqualified triumph can hardly be described.'
Within two months he was dead, a victim of tuberculosis

THEATRE ROYAL, COVENT-GARDEN.

LAST WEEK BUT ONE.

Grand Performance of Antient and Modern Music

Under the Management of

SIR GEORGE SMART.

A New and Splendid Orchestra,

On a novel Construction—designed and erected by Mr. E. SAUL, and decorated by Mr. LATILLA ; and

THE NEW ORGAN,

Built for the Theatre by Mr. Bishop, will be used for this Performance.

This present WEDNESDAY, MARCH 8, 1826,

PART I.......A SELECTION FROM

Der Freischütz,

UNDER THE DIRECTION OF THE COMPOSER,

CARL MARIA VON WEBER,

(Being his First Public Appearance in this Country.)

THE OVERTURE.

Chorus—Vittoria—MARCH
Air and Chorus, Mr. HORNCASTLE—Why good people.
Air, Mr. PHILLIPS—Haste nor lose.
Trio, Mr. BRAHAM, Mr. HORNCASTLE, Mr. ATKINS, and Chorus—Oh! how dark.
Scena, Mr. BRAHAM—Oh! I can bear my fate no longer.
Duet, Miss PATON, and Miss FARRAR—Come be gay.
The Bridesmaid's Song, Miss FARRAR—and Chorus—A bridal wreath.

Scena, Miss PATON—Softly sighs the voice of evening.
Chorus of Huntsmen—What equals on earth.
Trio, Miss PATON, Miss FARRAR, and Mr. BRAHAM, Where? what! oh, terror.
Finale—the Solo parts by Miss PATON, Miss H. CAWSE, Mr. BRAHAM, Mr. HORNCASTLE, Mr. ATKINS, Mr. TINNEY, and Chorus—See, O see.

At the End of Part I. (First time at these Performances.)

POT-POURRI for the CLARINET by Mr. RIBAS,

In which will be introduced the Air "*Je suis Lindor.*"....... *F. Danzi and Paesiello.*

PART II.

Aria, Madame VESTRIS——"*Una voce poco fà.*"......*Rossini.*

The following Selection from HANDEL's Sacred Oratorio,

JUDAS MACCABEUS.

To commence with the OVERTURE to ESTHER. *(Handel)*

Air, Miss FARRAR—Wise men flattering.
Recit. and Air, Mr. ATKINS—Arm, arm ye brave.
Chorus—We come.
Recit. and Air, Mr. BRAHAM—O Liberty.
(Accompanied on the Violoncello by Mr. Brooks.)
Air, Miss PATON—Come ever smiling Liberty.
Recit. Mr. HORNCASTLE—So will'd my father.
(with Double Choir) Mr. ROBINSON,
Air, LONGHURST, Mr. BRAHAM, Mr. HORNCASTLE,
Mr. ATKINS, Mr. TINNEY, & Chorus—Disdainful of danger.
Air, Mr. ATKINS—Haste we, my brethren.
Chorus—Hear us, O Lord.
Recit. and Air, Miss PATON—From mighty kings.

Recit. and Air, Mr. BRAHAM—Sound an alarm.
Chorus—We hear the pleasing dreadful call.
Recit. Mr. ATKINS—Ye worshippers of God.
Duet, Miss FARRAR and Miss H. CAWSE, O never bow we down.
Chorus—We never will bow down.
Recit. Mr. ATKINS—But lo! the conqueror comes.
Trio, Miss FARRAR, Mast. BARKER & Miss H. CAWSE, and
Duet, Miss PATON and Miss H. CAWSE—See the conquering hero.

MARCH.

Grand Chorus—Sing unto God.
The Solo parts by Mast. LONGHURST & Mr. HORNCASTLE.

PART III.

GRAND MISCELLANEOUS ACT.

First time at these Performances,) The admired *Chorus*, composed by MEYERBEER, in

IL CROCIATO IN EGITTO,

" *Dei Congiurati.*" (To which English words have been adapted.)
Song, Miss PATON—" Bonny brave Scotland,"
Air, Mr. BRAHAM, " Kelvin Grove."
Irish Ballad, Miss ROCHE, " Kathleen O'More,"......*arranged by C. Horn.*
Air, Madame VESTRIS, " Cherry ripe." C. Horn.
Echo Duet, Miss PATON and Mr. BRAHAM, " Now hope, now fear."......*Braham.*
Master BARKER, Master LONGHURST, Mr. ATKINS, & Chorus—" The Chough and Crow."—*Bishop.*
Duet, Miss FARRAR, and Miss H. CAWSE, " Tell pretty cousin." *Attwood.*
Grand Chorus,....(from *The Coronation Anthem*)—" God save the King."......*Handel.*

PRINCIPAL VOCAL PERFORMERS

Miss PATON,
AND
Madame VESTRIS,

Miss CAWSE,
Miss ROCHE,
(Her Second Performance at this Theatre)
Mr. ATKINS,
(First Performance at this Theatre.)
Mr. PHILLIPS,
Mast. LONGHURST,

Miss FARRAR,

Mr. HORNCASTLE,

Mast. BARKER,
Mr. ROBINSON,
AND
Mr. BRAHAM.

The BAND will be numerous and complete in every department,

Leader, Mr. MORI.

And the Choruses, under the superintendence of Mr. WATSON, will also be numerous, and will be assisted by the *Young Gentlemen of His Majesty's Chapel Royal,* and *St. Paul's Cathedral.*

Books of the Performance to be had in the Theatre, price 10d.——Places to be taken at the Box-Office, Hart-street.

*** The Dramatic Free List does not extend to this Performance.

Printed by W. Reynolds, Denmark Court, Strand.

NEVER ACTED.

Theatre Royal, Covent-Garden,

This present WEDNESDAY, April 12, 1826,

Will be performed (for the first time) a Grand Romantic and Fairy Opera, in three acts, (Founded on WIELAND's celebrated Poem) entitled

OBERON:
OR, THE ELF-KING's OATH.

With entirely new Music, Scenery, Machinery, Dresses and Decorations.

The OVERTURE and the whole of the MUSIC composed by

CARL MARIA VON WEBER,

Who will preside this Evening in the Orchestra.

The CHORUS (under the direction of Mr. WATSON,) has been greatly augmented.
The DANCES composed by Mr. AUSTIN.
The Scenery painted by Mess. GRIEVE, PUGH, T. and W. GRIEVE, LUPPINO, and assistants.
The Machinery by Mr. SAUL. Transformations & Decorations by Mess. BRADWELL.
The Dresses by Mr. PALMER.

Oberon, King of the Fairies, ... Miss SIDAS, and assistants.

Fairies
Puck, Miss H. CAWSE.
Titania, Queen of the Fairies, Miss SMITH.

Sir Huon, a Serenic Prince, Mr. BRAHAM,
Sherasmin, his Squire, Mr. FAWCETT.

Arabians
Charlemagne, Duke of Bouslesmen, Mr. CHAPMAN,
Babekan, a Saracen Prince, Mr. EVANS, Mr. J. ISAACS,
Haroun Al-Raschild, Caliph of Bagdad, Mr. ATKINS,
Almanzor, Emir of Tunis, Mr. AUSTIN, Miss PATON.

Tunisians
Roshana, Daughter of the Sultan, Mrs. DAVENPORT,
Namouna, Fatima's Grandmother, Mrs. VESTRIS,
Fatima, Reiza's Attendant, Mr. COOPER,
Reiza, Daughter of the Caliph, Miss LACY,
Abdallah, a Corsair, Mr. HORREBOW, Mr. TINNEY,
Roshana, a female slave, Miss WILSON,
Officers, Soldiers, Slaves, &c. of the different Courts—Fairies Sprites, &c.

Order of the Scenery

OBERON'S BOWER.
Painted by Mr. Grieve.
With the VISION.
By Sunset.
Distant View of Bagdad, and the adjacent Country on the Banks of the Tigris,
INTERIOR of RAMOUNA'S COTTAGE,
VESTIBULE and TERRACE in the HAREM of the CALIPH, overlooking the Tigris.
GRAND BANQUETTING CHAMBER of HAROUN
GARDENS of the PALACE.
PORT OF ASCALON.
Designed by Bradwell, and painted by Pugh.
RAVINE amongst the ROCKS of a DESOLATE ISLAND,
Perforated Cavern on the Beach,
The Haunt of the Spirits of the Storm.
With the OCEAN—in a STORM—and Moonlight.
Twilight—Starlight—and Moonlight.
Exterior of Gardener's House in the Pleasure Grounds of the Emir of Tunis.
Hall and Gallery in Almanzor's Palace.
MYRTLE GROVE in the GARDENS of the EMIR,
GOLDEN SALOON in the KIOSK of ROSHANA.
The Palace and Gardens by Moonlight.
COURT of the HAREM.
HALL of ARMS in the Palace of Charlemagne.

To which will be added (2d time) a NEW PIECE, in one act, called

THE SCAPE-GOAT.

Old Enricos, Mr. BLANCHARD, Charles, Mr. COOPER,
Ignatius Polyglot, Mr. W. FARREN, Robin, Mr. MEADOWS,
Molly Maggs, Miss JONES, Harriet, Miss A. JONES.

W. REYNOLDS, Printer, &c.

---

37 The First Night of Weber's *Oberon*, 12 April 1826

38 Weber's *Der Freischütz*, conducted by the composer on
8 March 1826

39 REGENCY 'swells' in the saloon at Covent Garden, 1821

40 MADAME VESTRIS (1787–1856) as the Goddess Diana in *Lionel and Clarissa*

41 FANNY KEMBLE (1809–93) as Juliet, 1829
The daughter of Charles Kemble, and the elder sister of Adelaide, her triumphant
first appearance as Juliet packed the theatre and saved her father from
bankruptcy. For the next three seasons her success was undiminished, with equal
acclaim for her performances both in tragedy and comedy. But like her sister her
career was short, for she married in 1834 and left the stage

Theatre Royal, Covent-Garden.

The Public is respectfully informed that THIS THEATRE

WILL BE OPENED

On MONDAY next, October 5, 1829.

When will be performed, Shakspeare's Tragedy of

ROMEO and JULIET.

Prince Escalus, Mr. HORREBOW,   Paris, Mr. DURUSET,
Montague, Mr. EVANS,   Capulet, Mr. EGERTON,
Romeo, -   Mr. ABBOTT,

(his first appearance at this Theatre these five years)

Mercutio, -   Mr. C. KEMBLE,

(his first appearance in that character)

Benvolio, Mr. BAKER,   Tybalt, Mr. DIDDEAR,   Friar John Mr. MEARS,
Friar Lawrence,   Mr. WARDE,

(his first appearance in that character)

Apothecary, Mr. MEADOWS,   Page Miss Fortescue,   Balthazar, Mr. Irwin
Abram Mr Heath, Samson Mr Atkins, Gregory Mr Norris, Peter, Mr. KEELEY

Juliet   by   Miss FANNY KEMBLE,

(Being her first appearance on any stage.)

Lady Capulet, *(on this occasion)* Mrs. C. KEMBLE,
Nurse,   Mrs. DAVENPORT,

In act I. a Masquerade and Dance

Incidental to the Piece.

In act V. The Funeral Procession of Juliet, and a Solemn Dirge.

The Vocal Parts by Mess. Ashton, Birt, Caulfield, Crumpton, Fuller, Goodson, Miller, May, Mears, Norris,
Purday, Shegog, G. Stansbury, C & S. Tett, Wood, &c. &c.
Mesdames Appleton, Brown, Cawse, H. Cawse, Clarke, Daly, Fenwick, Forde, Fortescue, Goodwin,
Keeley, Hughes, Hudson, Nicholson, Perry, Phillips, J. Scott, Weston, &c. &c.

To which will be added, the Melo-Drama of

The Miller & His Men.

Grindoff,   *(the Miller)*   Mr. FARLEY,
Count Friberg, Mr. HORREBOW,   Karl (his servant) Mr. BLANCHARD,   Lothair, Mr. DURUSET,
Kelmar (an old Cottager) Mr. EVANS,   Riber and Golotz (two Banditti) Mess. HENRY and MEARS,
Zingra, Mr. NORRIS,   Lindorf, Mr. S. TETT,   Coburg, Mr. FULLER,
Claudine,   Mrs. VINING,   Ravina, Miss LACY,

42 PLAYBILL announcing the debut of Fanny Kemble

44 POSTER for *Fidelio* (Beethoven), 12 June 1835, with Maria Malibran as Leonore

45 MALIBRAN'S debut at Covent Garden, 4 June 1830

43 MARIA MALIBRAN (1808–36)
Although born in Spain, the daughter of Manuel Garcia, a singing teacher, she was taken to Italy as a child; by the age of 15, she had lived in Naples, Paris and London. Her London debut, under her father's guidance, took place in 1825, and she was an immediate success. Her father pushed her into an unhappy marriage, and it was not until 1829 that she began her London career in earnest. Her appearances at Covent Garden were limited in number, for she spent much of her time in Belgium and in Italy with her future second husband. In what proved to be her final Covent Garden season, she appeared in *La Sonnambula*, prompting *The Times* critic to write:

The purity of her voice, the accuracy and facility of her execution, the profusion of gracefulness, and the intensity of feeling which she displays gives charms to the whole representation which seems to reach, as nearly as human genius can reach, the highest point of excellence (May 1835).

In April 1836, she fell from her horse while riding in London, and although she recovered, it was to prove a mortal injury: she died in Manchester in September the same year

46 MARIE TAGLIONI (1804–84) in *La Bayadère*

The daughter of the choreographer, Filippo Taglioni, who created *La Sylphide* for his daughter. On 26 July 1832 she appeared in the role for the first time at Covent Garden and astounded those who saw her, so different was she from the traditional dancers to whom they were accustomed. The *Morning Post* noted: 'all that the most poetical imagination could picture of sylph-like airiness.' Another writer remarked: 'She is all grace. . . . Though her face is not beautiful her figure is a perfect model. . . . She has attuned that form to the most delicate harmony, and her neck, her arms, and feet are all inspired by the same elegance.'

47 FANNY CERRITO (1817–1909)

Born in Naples, she made her debut in her native town in 1832, but she achieved her greatest successes in London: in her retirement in Paris she once told Thomas Cook, who was in Paris to make arrangements for his tourists, 'I love England and the English.' She first appeared in London at Covent Garden on 2 May 1840, before an audience which included Queen Victoria and her mother, the Duke of Wellington, and Prince Louis Napoleon, the future Emperor Napoleon III; a very athletic dancer, she amazed her audience by her languorous grace, and great lightness which made her seemingly float through the air. The greater part of her London career was spent at Her Majesty's Theatre, where Jules Perrot choreographed many works for her. In 1845 she married her most successful partner, Arthur Saint-Léon, but the marriage only lasted for six years. Frederick Gye attracted her back to Covent Garden for a season in 1855, and one of her final performances was once again before Queen Victoria and Napoleon III two years later

48 FANNY ELSSLER (1810–84)

The great rival of Marie Taglioni, she displayed both in her life and her art a peculiarly robust Viennese quality, very different from the ethereal Italian. Born the second daughter of Haydn's copyist, the composer paid for the education of both Thérèse and Fanny, until she entered the Hoftheater in 1818. In 1824 she was dancing in Naples where she had a son by the Prince of Salerno, whose favours she exchanged for those of Friedrich von Gentz when she returned to Vienna. Her name was even amorously linked with that of the Duke of Reichstadt. She made her London debut at the King's Theatre with her sister in 1833, in a city already won over by Taglioni; but her success in England was overshadowed by her reception in the United States where she toured in 1840–2. She was received by President Tyler and was acclaimed wherever she went. Thereafter, until her retirement in 1851 she danced all over the world, attracting a devoted following wherever she appeared. Théophile Gautier summed up the difference between her art and that of Taglioni, when he declared that while Taglioni was a 'Christian' dancer, Elssler was a 'pagan': in the energy and vibrancy of her dancing she had no rival

49 ADELAIDE KEMBLE (1814–79) as Norma,
2 November 1841

The tenure of Madame Vestris and her husband Charles Mathews at Covent Garden provided many artistic successes, but none greater than the introduction of the young Adelaide Kemble, the daughter of Charles Kemble. Sadly, her career ended with her marriage only two years later

50 ADELAIDE KEMBLE'S first appearance in *Norma* (Bellini),
2 November 1841

51 THE FIRST NIGHT of *London Assurance*. Both Madame Vestris and her husband Charles Mathews took leading roles, and the play ran for fifty-nine nights

52 DION DE BOUCICAULT (1822–90) and his wife, the Scottish actress, AGNES ROBERTSON

His first play, *London Assurance*, was an overnight success at Covent Garden in May 1841

53 HENRY ROWLEY BISHOP (1786–1855)
The Musical Director of Covent Garden for thirteen years, from
1811, he experienced the theatre at the height of its success under
J. P. Kemble as well as its steady decline under the motley
succession of managements which followed him. But his own
reputation lies in his compositions, with over eighty operas and
many airs to his credit, among them 'Home Sweet Home' and
'Cherry Ripe'. That Bishop was the first musician ever to receive a
knighthood (1842) owed not a little to Queen Victoria's liking for
his more sentimental productions

54 SIR MICHAEL COSTA (1808–84)
Born in Naples, the son of a composer,
he first came to London in 1830,
engaged as a *maestro al piano* at the
King's Theatre. He composed the music
for many ballets, and became a great
figure in the London musical world. In
1846 he was offered the conductorship
of the Philharmonic Society. The
manager of the King's Theatre,
Benjamin Lumley, refused him
permission to take up the post; Costa
resigned and emerged in the following
year at the new Royal Italian Opera at
Covent Garden. Costa attracted the
leading singers of the day to the new
theatre, and his standard of conducting,
together with the musical quality he
imparted to his orchestras, made him
one of the foremost musical figures of
the age

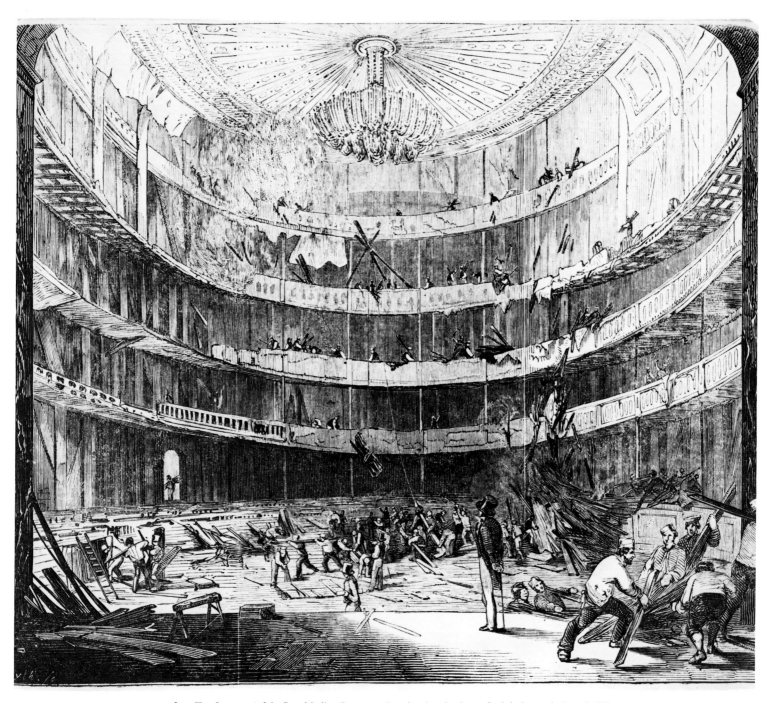

55, 56, 57 The Interior of the Royal Italian Opera, 1846–7, showing the theatre both before and after rebuilding
Benedict Albano, the architect of the new Italian opera, took possession of the theatre in December 1846. For five
weeks up to 2,000 workmen, working 24 hours a day, gutted the old theatre and constructed an entirely new interior
ready for opening in April 1847. The new auditorium was dominated by a vast gaselier, which made the upper reaches
of the theatre unbearably hot

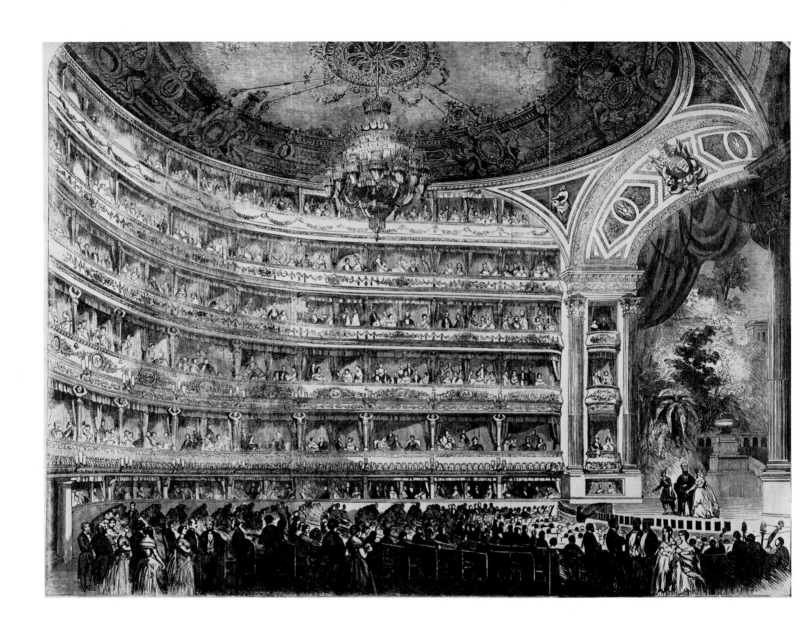

58 *Lucrezia Borgia* (Donizetti), performed for the first time at Covent Garden on 15 May 1847, with Mario as Gennaro, Grisi as Lucrezia, and Alboni as Maffio Orsini

59 FANNY PERSIANI (1812–67)

She first played a leading role on the stage of a little theatre built by her father, Nicolò Tacchinardi near Florence, but she did not make her professional debut until 1832 at Leghorn; two years before she had married the composer Giuseppe Persiani. Her rise after her first performance was rapid: Donizetti wrote *Lucia di Lammermoor* for her in 1835. She first appeared in London as Amina in *La Sonnambula* (Bellini), and from 1838 she sang alternately in London and Paris. In appearance she was dowdy, but she developed an exquisite sensitivity in her singing which moved audiences deeply. In 1843 she overstrained her voice while singing in London, and the edge was taken off the quality of her performance, although she had successful London seasons in the years 1847–9

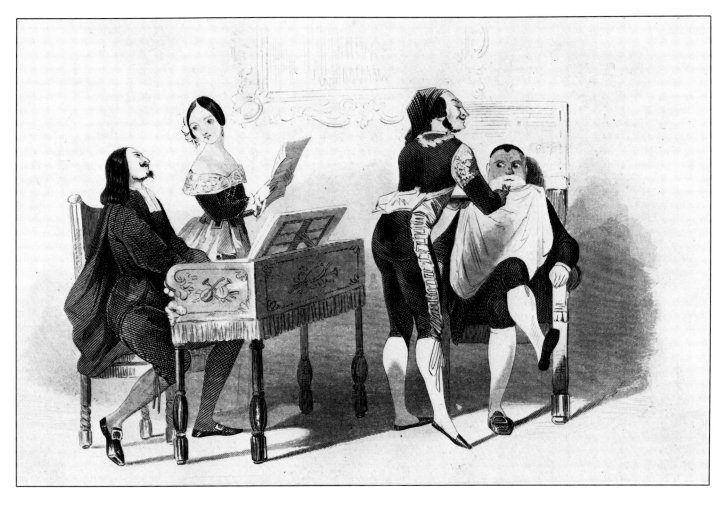

60 THE FIRST PERFORMANCE in Italian of *Il Barbiere di Siviglia*
(Rossini) at the Royal Italian Opera on 1 June 1847. Fanny
Persiani took the part of Rosina, Giorgio Ronconi that of Figaro,
with Agostino Rovere as Dr Bartolo and Luigi Salvi as Count
Almaviva

61 GIOVANNI MARIO (1810–83), in the title role of *Masaniello*

Auber's *Masaniello*, with Dorus-Gras as Elvira was the opening
production of the 1849 season. Mario, the son of an Italian
general, from a noble family, was tempted from a promising
military career to the operatic stage by the director of the Paris
Opéra, who recognized his fine voice and great dramatic presence.
He made his London debut in 1839, and in 1845 he settled down
with the great singer Giulia Grisi, a partnership only broken by
her death in 1869. Like so many singers who earned huge sums at
the peak of their career, Mario ended his life in poverty, in Rome

62 QUEEN VICTORIA and PRINCE ALBERT arrive at Covent Garden on
10 July 1851 for a performance of *Il Flauto magico* by Mozart. The Queen was
not, however, impressed: 'The opera itself was performed in a most slovenly
manner. The 3 black ladies sang very badly, the scenery etc., very inferior and
Mario only really walked through his part.'

63 FREDERICK GYE (1809–78)

Gye was, after Rich, the most enterprising and successful of all the managers of Covent Garden. The son of an impresario, for his father was the proprietor of the Vauxhall Gardens, his association with Covent Garden lasted for over thirty years. After 1847 the theatre flourished in its new guise of the Royal Italian Opera; it was much favoured by Queen Victoria, and Gye was successful in introducing many new works and singers to English audiences. But his greatest qualities, of determination and invincible spirit, only became clear in the catastrophe of the theatre's destruction by fire in 1856. After the disaster, which had destroyed almost all his available assets, he mounted a season at the Lyceum Theatre within a month of the fire. By this means he kept his company together while he sought financial backing to rebuild Covent Garden. The company played for two seasons at the Lyceum, and during this time he raised the huge sum of £120,000 to rebuild the theatre, and to re-equip it on the scale he believed necessary. When the splendid new opera house re-opened in May 1858, Gye was faced with continuing financial problems, which were only gradually resolved: by his death in 1878, the opera house was making a substantial annual profit. Gye had a sure sense of what the public wanted, and he deliberately set out to make Covent Garden the leading theatre of the capital. It was tragic that he died by accident, victim of a stray shot in a shooting party at Dytchley Park, near Oxford, while at the height of his success. His son had little of his father's restless energy and commercial shrewdness, and it was not until Augustus Harris occupied Gye's place that the theatre was once more in capable hands

64 *Fidelio* (Beethoven) performed at Covent Garden in 1851, with Enrico Tamberlik as Floristan. Tamberlik (1820–89), was of Turkish origin although educated in Italy, where he first appeared in Rome in 1837. His first performance on the London stage took place in 1850

65 THE FIRST NIGHT of *Il Trovatore*,
10 May 1855

66 PAULINE VIARDOT (1821–1910)
The youngest child of the Spanish
singer and composer, Manuel Garcia,
early in her career she was
overshadowed by the success of her
elder sister Maria Malibran. She sang
at Covent Garden 1848–51 and
1854–5

67 THE GRAND STAIRCASE at Covent Garden.
This was one of the many evenings when a Bal Masqué was held,
a tradition which lasted until the First World War

68 M. Jullien's Grand Bal Masqué at Covent Garden, 9 March 1844

Louis Jullien originated the notion of the Promenade Concert with a series of spectacular productions at Covent Garden, and expanded the popular entertainment of the *bal masqué* into a huge costume ball. It was after one such event given by Henry Anderson on 4 March 1856 that the theatre burned down; this setback delayed but did not quench Jullien's plans for further extravaganzas. But financial reality caught up with him, and he died a pauper in a mental hospital. He possessed, as one obituary noted, 'unbounded energy, vision, and unlimited confidence in himself.'

On Wednesday morning, one of the most terrible conflagrations that has occurred in the metropolis for a long period, broke out at the Theatre Royal, Covent Garden, during the progress of Professor Anderson's bal masqué.

At twenty minutes to five o'clock the company had dwindled to about 200 persons on the stage or ball room, and the orchestra were in the act of playing the concluding bars of the National Anthem when a large portion of one of the fly scenes fell suddenly on the stage, a few paces in front of the ordinary position of the stage lights. Several persons narrowly escaped injury from the falling mass; but the alarm created by this circumstance had not subsided when sparks descending from the roof above the stage spread terror throughout the assembly. Those who only an instant before had been indulging in the giddy dance, were now shrieking for help, and flying to the several exit doors in the hope of saving their lives.

There was no time for thought or consideration. In a few seconds the interior of the building was full of dense black smoke, and the greatest possible alarm for individual safety was felt on every side. The utmost confusion and consternation prevailed. The masquers left the theatre in a state of the most perfect terror, while the flames were ascending high above them into the air.

A vain attempt was made to rescue some of the properties of the theatre, and, among the rest, the machinery appending to Mr. Anderson's tricks; but this, of course, was perfectly fruitless. The cash-box, however, was among the first of the articles carried out of the theatre.

Mr. Braidwood, with his fire-brigade, were early in attendance; but from the first he saw that all hope of saving any part of the theatre was futile, and the exertions of twenty engines were exclusively devoted to throwing water on the surrounding property, and preventing the fire from extending to Covent-garden Market on the west, and Bow Street on the east. This was done, but nothing beyond. Of the theatre not a vestige is saved—nothing but the bare walls are left of that superb temple, which, under the management of Mr. Gye, had become world-famous as the seat of music and of song.

69–70 Panic Ensues with the outbreak of fire during the Bal Masqué on the
night of 4 March 1856

72 QUEEN VICTORIA visits the ruins in March 1856 in the company
of Frederick Gye

73 THE smouldering ruins of the theatre

71 THE DESTRUCTION of the
Theatre Royal, Covent Garden,
by fire on the morning
of 5 March 1856

The World's Greatest Theatre

IN THE EIGHTY-ONE YEARS between the opening of the third theatre and the outbreak of the Second World War most of the greatest singers of the day appeared there and many of the greatest operas ever written were performed.

74 (PREVIOUS PAGE) THE THEATRE ROYAL, Covent Garden, seen from Bow Street, with the Floral Hall to one side, 1861

75 THE FIRST NIGHT of the Royal Italian Opera, 15 May 1858, in the new theatre, rebuilt after the fire

76 THE CRUSH BAR of the Royal Italian Opera, 1858

77 Poster for *Un Ballo in Maschera*

78 The First Covent Garden production of *Un Ballo in Maschera* (Verdi), 1861,
conducted by Michael Costa

79 BARRY's new theatre at Covent
Garden, May 1858

80 THE 'CONSERVATORY' or Floral Hall
attached to the Opera House, 1857

Designed by E. M. Barry, this was never
a great success, either as a flower
market, for which it was never used, or
as a concert hall. It was eventually put
to use as a fruit and vegetable market
until it was destroyed by fire

82 THEODOR WACHTEL (1823–93)
as Manrico in *Il Trovatore* (Verdi)

Wachtel began life as a Hamburg cab
driver, but his powerful voice soon
provided the entrée into the world of
opera. He was a rather wooden
performer, remarkable more for the
force of his singing than its beauty. He
first appeared at Covent Garden in 1862,
with Manrico being one of his most
successful parts

81 PAULINE LUCCA (1841–1908)

By birth a Viennese, of Italian parents, her vocal gifts were first
recognised in the choir of the Karlskirche in Vienna, where she
once took the principal singer's part at short notice. She appeared
at Berlin in 1861, encouraged by Meyerbeer who had no doubts
about her talent: she was rapidly appointed a Court Singer, for life.
When she first came to Covent Garden in 1863, her performance
in *Les Huguenots* (Meyerbeer) created a sensation. Thereafter she
appeared regularly at Covent Garden, in a variety of operas, by
Gounod, Mozart and Bizet; her reputation was even higher in
Russia, where she took St Petersburg by storm, and in the United
States. But in later life she settled in Vienna as the leading figure
of the Court Opera until her retirement in 1889. Her performances
as Marguerite in *Faust* (Gounod) and in *Carmen* (Bizet) were
considered unsurpassed by many who saw them

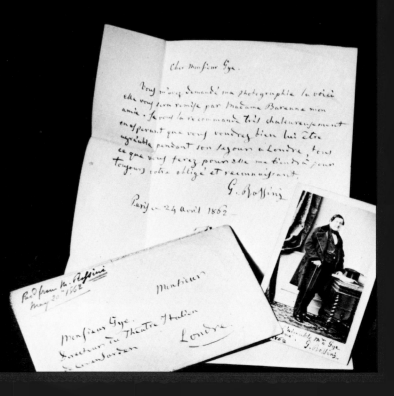

83 A LETTER and photograph from Rossini to Frederick Gye at
the Royal Italian Opera

THE INCOMPARABLE PATTI

84–86 ADELINA PATTI (1843–1919)
Perhaps the greatest coloratura singer of
her age, and the successor of Giulia
Grisi as the *doyenne* of the Covent
Garden stage, Adelina Patti was born
into a family of singers. Throughout her
long career she possessed a voice of
great purity which, coupled with true
dramatic sensitivity, made her a
remarkable artist. From her first
performance at Covent Garden in May
1861 she was recognised as an
incomparable performer, and it was the
lure of her name which drew audiences
to the opera. She appeared in every
season from 1861 to 1884, and when she
returned for a farewell season in 1895,
the response was tumultuous. The critic
Herman Klein noted: 'Society was fairly
agog in anticipation of an experience
whereof the most brilliant Melba or de
Reszke night never furnished more than
a faint replica.' She loved her adopted
country, and took out British citizenship
in 1898; at her castle, *Craig y nos*, near
Swansea, she built a private theatre.
There she performed in her retirement,
emerging into the wider world for an
occasional recital. In 1914 she appeared
in a concert in aid of the Red Cross.
When she sang 'Home, sweet home', to
a hushed audience, it was clear that even
in her seventies, her voice had lost none
of its legendary freshness and precision

84 As Marguerite in *Faust* (Gounod)

85 As Catherine in *L'Etoile du Nord* (Meyerbeer)

86 As Leonora in *Il Trovatore* (Verdi)

87 THÉRÈSE TIETJENS (1831–77) as Lucrezia in *Lucrezia Borgia*

In a career which began in 1848, Tietjens rapidly became a singer of
international reputation. She appeared at Covent Garden in 1869 and 1870, and
identified closely with the role of Lucrezia. In her later years she became grossly
fat with the cancer which was to kill her, and when taken ill in Dublin, she is said
to have declared: 'If I am to die, I will play Lucrezia once more.'

88 VICTOR MAUREL (1848–1923), as Iago in *Otello* (Verdi), 1889

One of his finest roles, Iago was first presented on the London stage in 1889. He returned in 1895 to present it at Covent Garden for the first time. The French baritone's major triumphs came in roles where his acting talents were allowed full play, as in his Falstaff which achieved an instant success at Covent Garden in the same year. He also appeared in a number of non-operatic productions, and showed himself to be an accomplished and subtle performer

89 POL PLANÇON (1854–1914) as St Bris in *Les Huguenots* (Meyerbeer)

The noted French singer made his debut in this role at Lyons in 1877. He first appeared at Covent Garden in 1891, and such was his popular appeal that he returned in every season until 1904

90 SIR AUGUSTUS HARRIS (1852–96)

A theatrical impresario of genius, Augustus Harris was associated with the theatre almost from birth: his father was stage manager at Covent Garden. In later life Harris recalled: 'Almost as soon as I could run alone he used to take me with him to the theatre. I remember quite well, as a little boy, standing in the wings as he walked about the stage, while the great prima donnas came and petted and kissed me.' He became manager of Drury Lane in 1879, where he showed his skill and capacity to make a profit. In 1889, supported by some of the leading figures in society, he rented the Covent Garden theatre. In the four years that followed, he introduced a torrent of changes at the opera house. French and German operas were now heard in their original language: he brought a young Australian singer named Melba to the theatre, and he created the opera as the social centre of the London scene, with the Royal patronage of the Prince and Princess of Wales. Under Harris's guidance the Royal Opera House (as it was known from 1892) achieved the eminence of a great international theatre

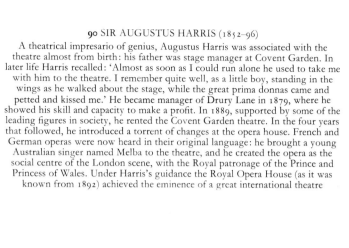

91 THE MAIN FRONT of the Royal Opera House in 1896, completed in 1858 by E. M. Barry

93 EDOUARD DE RESZKE (left),
(1853–1917), with his brother Jean
(right) en route to New York, 1890s

Both the de Reszkes were popular
figures on the London operatic stage;
Edouard appeared in each season from
1888 to the turn of the century. Taller
than Jean, he seemed a larger figure on
stage; his voice had volume and great
resonance, which, coupled with a fine
sense of acting, made him an
outstanding operatic bass

92 JEAN DE RESZKE (1850–1925) as Lohengrin

One of the great figures at Covent Garden in the 1890s, Jean de Reszke was born
into a prominent Polish family; his mother was a successful amateur musician,
and she influenced not only Jean, but his brother Edouard and his sister
Josephine to take up careers on the operatic stage. He first appeared at Drury
Lane, but his reputation in England was based on his many performances at
Covent Garden, from 1888 onwards. He was a splendid actor, with a repertoire
which covered much of the operatic canon, but it was in the great Wagnerian
roles that he was at his peak

94 EMMA ALBANI (1847–1930)

A Canadian soprano, she moved with her family to Albany, New York. When
her talents became clear a public collection raised the money to send her for
study in Europe: she took the stage name of Albani out of gratitude to her
adopted city. In 1878, she married Ernest Gye, the eldest son of the manager of
Covent Garden; in the following year Ernest Gye took over as the manager of
the theatre. A singer of considerable talent, she specialised in Wagnerian roles,
and last appeared at Covent Garden in 1911, thirty-nine years after her debut in
the theatre. Her Isolde of 1896, her final full season, with Jean de Reszke as
Tristan, was 'the last and greatest triumph of her career'

95 DR HANS RICHTER (1843–1916)

Richter's position as the supreme exponent of the music of Richard Wagner for over forty years was based on his deep knowledge of the works and of the composer himself. As a young man he worked with Wagner, making the definitive fair copies of *Die Meistersinger* and the *Ring*. He conducted at Bayreuth and at many of the first performances of Wagner's work throughout Europe. He gave the first series of Wagner concerts at the Albert Hall in 1877, sharing the conducting with Wagner himself. In 1870, he presented the first Wagner opera at Drury Lane, and five years later the first at Covent Garden. He stamped his style and personality on Wagner productions at Covent Garden for over twenty years, but his influence ran wider than the purely German repertoire. He developed an admiration for the work of Elgar, and did much to promote his work, including the Elgar Festival held at Covent Garden in 1904. He took pride in promoting the careers of English singers, and of the Hallé Orchestra which he conducted. His last production was of *Die Meistersinger* at Bayreuth in 1911, where he spent his last years. Richter was a powerful and combative figure, and it was largely through his efforts that Wagner's works achieved proper recognition on the English operatic stage

96 THE 1892 production of *Götterdämmerung* which was conducted by Gustav Mahler, then aged 32

97 FAFNER'S CAVE from 1892 *Siegfried*

98 THE German opera season at Covent Garden, 1892

ROYAL OPERA
COVENT GARDEN
The Grand Opera Syndicate, Ld.
Lessees
Managing Director - - Mr. MAURICE GRAU

STATE
PERFORMANCE

WEDNESDAY
JUNE 23, 1897, at 8.45

TO COMMEMORATE THE SIXTIETH ANNIVERSARY OF HER MAJESTY'S
ACCESSION TO THE THRONE

Programme

"GOD SAVE THE QUEEN"
SUNG BY THE PRINCIPAL ARTISTS AND THE FULL CHORUS

TANNHÄUSER
Act 2

HERMANN I.	...	...	M. PLANÇON	BITEROLF	...	...	M. GILIBERT
TANNHÄUSER	...	...	M. VAN DYCK	HEINRICH	...	...	M. PAZ
WOLFRAM	...	...	M. RENAUD	REINMAR	...	...	M. MEUX
WALTHER	...	...	M. BONNARD	ELIZABETH	...	...	MME. EMMA EA

Conductor - M. ANTON SEIDL

ROMEO ET JULIETTE
Act 3

CAPULET	...	M. PLANÇON			
ROMEO	...	M. JEAN DE RESZKE	GERTRUDE	...	MLLE.
FRÈRE LAURENT	...	M. EDOUARD DE RESZKE	JULIETTE	...	MME.

Conductor - Signor MANCINELLI

LES HUGUENOTS
Act 4

COMTE DE ST. BRIS	...	M. PLANÇON		
VALENTINE	...	Miss MACINTYRE	COMTE DE NEVERS	...
			RAOUL DE NANGIS	...

Conductor - M. FLON

Stage Manager: Mr. T. H. FRIEND.   Secretary & Business Manager: Mr. NEIL FO

101 A DINNER given by Neil Forsyth, the secretary of the Grand Opera Syndicate, in the theatre, 1906. Present are most of the members of the board of directors and the guests include Lady de Grey, the driving force behind their deliberations

99 THE SILK PROGRAMME commemorating Queen Victoria's Diamond Jubilee, 23 June 1897

100 A COMMAND PERFORMANCE of Mascagni's *Cavalleria Rusticana* at Windsor Castle in the presence of HM Queen Victoria, 26 November 1891

The Queen's frequent visits to the opera ended with the death of the Prince Consort in 1861 and the virtual seclusion she imposed upon herself. Although she never again appeared in a public theatre or concert hall, she fulfilled a great love of music by arranging for the leading artists of the day to appear before her in private. Patti came in July 1872, to the Queen's evident delight: 'I was charmed with Patti, who has a very sweet voice, and wonderful facility and execution . . . her rendering of *Home, Sweet Home* was touching beyond measure, and quite brought tears to one's eyes.' Of male singers, her special favourites were Jean and Edouard de Reszke, who appeared before her in several performances, including a production of *Lohengrin* in celebration of her 80th birthday.

The Waterloo Chamber at Windsor Castle is still used for concerts

102 EDWARD ELGAR (1857–1934) in the music room of his house, *c.* 1915
Dr Hans Richter was both a friend and passionate enthusiast for Elgar's music, and it was at his insistence that an Elgar Festival was held at Covent Garden in 1904

103 THE DIVINE MELBA (1861–1931)

104 THE STARS of the Grand Opera season, 1907

105 THE GERMAN OPERA season of 1908 was a triumph for Percy Pitt and Dr Hans Richter, but Richter's other great plan, to produce opera in English in the 'grand seasons', was turned down. The Chairman of the Grand Opera Syndicate, Harry Higgins, was unambiguous:

My conviction is that there is very little demand in England for opera at all outside the season, and that outside the small circle of those who have an axe of their own to grind, the idea that a craving exists for opera to be given in English is an absolute delusion.

106 EMMY DESTINN, as Tess, in D'Erlanger's opera *Tess*, at Covent Garden, 1909–10

The great Czech soprano (1878–1930) made her Covent Garden debut in 1904; such was her success that she appeared every season until the First World War. When she returned to the London stage in 1919 something of the youthful sparkle had vanished

107 ENRICO CARUSO (1873–1921)

108 LUISA TETRAZZINI (1871–1940)

She arrived in London as a virtual unknown in the autumn of 1907, pressed upon a reluctant management by her brother-in-law, the conductor Campanini. So poor were the advance bookings that attempts were made to cancel her debut, but she would have none of it. When the performance came she won round an apathetic audience, so that by the end of *La Traviata* the applause was rapturous. No actress, and stocky in appearance, the magic of her performance lay in her brilliant vocalisation

109 DINH GILLY (1877–1940) as the
Sheriff, Jack Rance, in *La Fanciulla del
west (The Girl of the Golden West)*
(Puccini), Covent Garden, May 1911

Puccini's opera came to London some
six months after its New York premiere:
it was an instant popular success which
sold out within an hour of the box office
opening. Emmy Destinn and the French
baritone Dinh Gilly were given a
rapturous reception: 'Puccini and the
cast were recalled countless times at the
end of the evening.' Gilly became a
regular visitor to Covent Garden. He
settled in England and married an
English singer: his daughter, Renée,
sang Carmen at Covent Garden in 1937

110 MADAMA BUTTERFLY, Summer 1911.
Emmy Destinn, seen here as Cio-Cio-
San, appeared in the first British
performance, at Covent Garden in 1905

111 MAGGIE TEYTE (1888–1976), as
Cherubino in *The Marriage of Figaro*,
2 November 1910, the year of her
Covent Garden debut

112–113–115 SIR THOMAS BEECHAM (1879–1961): three
faces of a musical autocrat

114 THE SECOND Beecham season at Covent Garden, 1910

116 RICHARD STRAUSS (1864–1949), who first conducted in
London in 1897, returned in 1910 for the last two performances of
his opera *Elektra* at Covent Garden, conducting performances on
12 and 15 March. The *Observer* described the opera as 'The sternest
entertainment ever offered to mortal man'

THE OPERA THAT WILL "ELEKTRIFY" LONDON.

TO SING THE MOST ARDUOUS SCORE EVER WRITTEN: CHARACTERS IN STRAUSS'S "ELEKTRA,"
TO BE PRODUCED FOR THE FIRST TIME AT COVENT GARDEN ON SATURDAY.

117 *Elektra*, by Richard Strauss, first appeared in London on 19 February 1910, under the baton of Thomas Beecham. Like *Salome*, where the Lord Chamberlain had intervened to prevent the head of St John the Baptist being carried on a charger—with the consequence that Salome sang to an empty dish—*Elektra* aroused an angry and turbulent response. With *Der Rosenkavalier*, the Lord Chamberlain intervened again, prohibiting the bed on stage in the third act

118 MARIA JERITZA, A Czech soprano of great beauty and presence, she was chosen by Strauss to create the role of Ariadne in *Ariadne auf Naxos* at Stuttgart in 1912; her first appearance in London at Covent Garden was a triumph, with all seats sold. As Tosca, her voice 'was beautiful, powerful, and delicate in turns.'

119 NIJINSKY in *L'Après-midi d'un faune*, presented by Serge Diaghilev at
Covent Garden, 1912

120 CostUME by Léon Bakst for Nijinsky in *Le Dieu bleu*, 1911, now on permanent display in the Royal Opera House

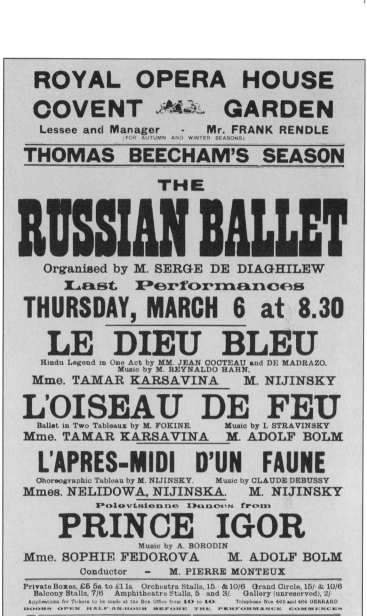

121 The DiAGHILEV ballet season of 1911 which introduced the Russian style of ballet to British audiences

122 SARAH BERNHARDT (1845–1923), whose voice was 'like the silver sound of running water', appeared only once at Covent Garden, in the company of Mrs Patrick Campbell, Clara Butt, Anna Pavlova, Gertie Millar and Vesta Tilley, in aid of the Titanic Disaster Fund, May 1912. The programme sellers, drawn from the ranks of society, were marshalled by Lady Alexander and Lady Beerbohm Tree; among them was the young Lady Diana Manners (later Lady Diana Cooper)

123 TAMARA KARSAVINA (1885–1978)
The first and the greatest of Diaghilev's ballerinas, she had by 1909 become the star of the Maryinsky Ballet, set in
Theatre Street in St Petersburg, about which she wrote in her autobiography *Theatre Street*. She came with Diaghilev
to Paris and to London, dancing Armide in the first appearance of the Russian ballet at Covent Garden in 1911. She
married an English diplomat and came to live in London in 1917, and played thereafter an important role in the
development of ballet in Britain

124 ANTONIO SCOTTI (1866–1936)
as Scarpia in *Tosca* (Puccini), 1914
A native of Naples, he played Scarpia in the first Covent Garden
production of *Tosca* in 1900, a role to which he returned in five
subsequent seasons and his final season of 1914. All who saw him
were convinced that they had heard a great singer, and one of the
defining interpretations of the role

125 JOHN McCORMACK (1884–1943)
He made his debut in 1907 as Turiddu in Mascagni's *Cavalleria
Rusticana* and returned each year until 1914

126 FEODOR CHALIAPIN (1873–1938)

Chaliapin combined two elemental forces in his performances: a brooding dramatic power, and a voice of strength and resonance. These qualities dictated the roles which he could undertake: his presentations of Ivan the Terrible and Boris Godunov have never been equalled. Born a peasant in Kazan, he was a man of wide learning. He played a number of instruments, wrote prose and verse, and translated Boito's *Mefistofeles*—another of his favourite roles—into Russian. In addition to his operatic performances he loved the folk songs of his native Russia, and recorded a number of them. He remained a man of the people, and recalled his visit to the Worker's House in Kharkov in 1904:

I had long wanted to sing to ordinary simple people, the people I came from. . . . It was inspiring, I had begun singing at four in the afternoon, and without noticing the time or even feeling tired went on singing. . . . Before I left I asked the workers to join in with me. First we sang 'Down the Volga' but somehow it didn't fit in with the mood, and I then suggested 'Dubinushka', which they did with enormous enthusiasm.

He appeared at Drury Lane before the First World War, but it was not until 1926 that he appeared, as Mefistofeles (see left), at Covent Garden

To Covent Garden:
In memory of my
world premiere of
La Traviata
Rosa Ponselle

127–128 ROSA PONSELLE (1897–1981), as Violetta in *La Traviata* (Verdi), 1930
Born in America of immigrant Italian parents, she was one of the great singers to be identified with the Metropolitan Opera in New York. She appeared as a regular visitor at Covent Garden, and her Violetta was hailed as 'an alliance between first-class singing and first-class intelligence'

The Camargo Ballet Society

by arrangement with the Government Hospitality Fund and by
the courtesy of the Covent Garden Opera Syndicate, (1930) Ltd.

presents

TWO GALA PERFORMANCES

of

Ballet

at the

Royal Opera, Covent Garden

on

Tuesday, June 27 and Thursday, June 29 at 9.15 p.m.

in honour of the

World Economic Conference

when it is hoped that the principal
delegates of the Assembled Powers will
be present as the guests of the Society.

The programme, which will be arranged with the assistance of

The Vic-Wells Ballet

by permission of Miss Lilian Baylis, C.H., M.A. Oxon. (Hon.)
will be as follows:—

COPPELIA

Music by DELIBES

SPECTRE DE LA ROSE

Music by WEBER

LAC DES CYGNES

Music by TSCHAIKOVSKY

PRINCIPAL DANCERS:

THAMAR KARSAVINA,   ANTON DOLIN,
LYDIA LOPOKOVA,   STANLEY JUDSON,
NINETTE DE VALOIS,   HEDLEY BRIGGS,
ALICIA MARKOVA,   FREDERICK ASHTON
URSULA MORETON,

Conductors:

SIR THOMAS BEECHAM

CONSTANT LAMBERT

For Prices, see over.

129 THE CAMARGO SOCIETY (named after the great French dancer
of the eighteenth century) was founded in 1930. It aimed to
present ballet to subscription audiences, and in special galas (as
here). It drew its dancers in the main from the groups organised
by Marie Rambert and Ninette de Valois. In the three years of the
Society's existence (1930–3) some sixteen new ballets were
produced

130 IDA RUBINSTEIN (1885–1960) in *Le Martyre de Saint-
Sébastien*, July 1931

Born in St Petersburg, she studied under Fokine and joined
Diaghilev where she created the chief roles in *Cléopatre* and
Schéhérezade. A remarkably fine actress and character dancer, she
formed her own company in 1928, in which many notable young
dancers appeared, including Frederick Ashton

131 FREDERICK ASHTON,
in a studio portrait as Pierrot in
Carnaval, 1935

Mathilde Kchesinska

The Great Ballerina in Her

Covent Garden "Danse Boyard"

Mathilde Kchesinska's appearance at Covent Garden with the de Basil Company was a great ballet occasion. She last danced there in 1911, and since those days all the glittering background of her brilliant career as prima ballerina absoluta of Imperialist Russia has vanished. It is impossible to believe Kchesinska is sixty-three, either off the stage or in the traditional character piece, "Danse Boyard," which she chose for her short solo. She and her husband, the Grand Duke Andrew, now live in Paris where she teaches ballerinas—present and to come (Riabouchinska is one of her pupils). Before she went back last week, she gave the Vic-Wells ballet company their first lesson after their holiday; this was her contribution, and an extremely interesting one, to the Vic-Wells Five Year Plan to create a national school of ballet.

Irina Baronova

Ballerina of Colonel de Basil's

Ballets Russes

TO see Baronova dance (Arnold Haskell calls her the "most poetical of modern ballerinas"), to be held spellbound by the beauty and passion of her *pas de deux* with Lichine in *Présages*, and then to remember that, if she wasn't a dancer, she'd be just a schoolgirl of sixteen, is to believe once and for all in the ageless miracle of the ballet. Baronova, known as the baby of the company, is a pupil of Olga Preobrajenska's famous studio in Paris, made her début when Colonel de Basil opened his first season in Monte Carlo in 1931, and appeared in London for the first time in 1933 at the Alhambra. Here she is photographed in *Le Spectre de la Rose*, one of her loveliest parts, in contrast to the profundity of feeling in her dancing in this and *Présages*, her versatility includes the gaiety and a kind of serene humour for such characters as the jealous Top in *Jeux d'Enfants*, the vamp in *Union Pacific*, and the charming little soubrette in *Beau Danube*.

132 MATHILDA KSCHESSINSKA (1872–1971)
The doyenne of the Russian Imperial ballet, and a former mistress of Czar Nicholas II, Kschessinska was the only Russian *prima ballerina assoluta*; she married, morganatically, into the Imperial family. She danced for the Diaghilev company in Paris in 1909, and thereafter appeared regularly in the West. She last appeared on the London stage in the de Basil Ballets Russes season. A woman of great wealth and talent, she died in her ninety-ninth year, the last point of contact with the splendours of the Russian ballet in the 1890s

133 IRINA BARONOVA
When Colonel de Basil brought his Ballets Russes to London in 1932, he brought with him the 'baby ballerinas'—Irina Baronova and Tatiana Riabouchinska, together with Tamara Toumanova. The brilliance of their dancing did much to ensure the success of the early de Basil seasons

134 TATIANA RIABOUCHINSKA
playing the Golden Cockerel in
Le Coq d'Or, with the de Basil company
at Covent Garden, 1937

135 LOTTE LEHMANN (1888–1976) as Leonore in *Fidelio* (Beethoven), 30 April 1934

136 *Il Barbiere di Siviglia* (Rossini) performed in the Imperial League of Opera season at Covent Garden, 1935, with Leon Ponzio as Figaro and Heddle Nash as Count Almaviva

The Imperial League of Opera was formed by Sir Thomas Beecham in the 1920s and presented three seasons of opera at Covent Garden in the 1930s

137 QUEEN MARY visiting the opera, 12 March 1935, to see
Grace Moore, who had appeared in the film *One Night of Love*, in
her first London operatic performance in *La Bohème* (Puccini). The
singer caused many ruffled feathers among the musical
establishment

138 LAURITZ MELCHIOR (1890–1973) as Lohengrin, 1935
Born in Denmark, Melchior appeared regularly at Covent Garden.
He made many Wagner appearances, singing Tristan over 200
times

139 KIRSTEN FLAGSTAD (1895–1962) as Isolde, 1936

140 GIOVANNI MARTINELLI (1885–1969), as Otello, 1937
His appearance in this role was triumphantly successful, as was his
performance in *Turandot* in the same season, hailed as being 'full of
exquisite subtleties'. He had first appeared at Covent Garden
twenty-five years before, when he showed the elegance and vocal
polish which was to be the hallmark of his career

141 DAVID LICHINE (1910–72) as The Blue Bird, in *Le Mariage d'Aurore*,
1 July 1937
Lichine was one of the many fine dancers who came to London with the de Basil
company

142 LÉONIDE MASSINE (1885–1979)
dancing in *Schéhérezade* at Covent
Garden, 9 July 1935

143 'Princesses at the pantomime': Princess Elizabeth and
Princess Margaret at *Red Riding Hood*, Covent Garden, February
1939

144 MARIA CANIGLIA and BENIAMINO GIGLI (1890–1957)
in *La Traviata* (Verdi), May 1939

145 ROBERT HELPMANN and
MARGOT FONTEYN in *The Sleeping
Princess*, March 1939

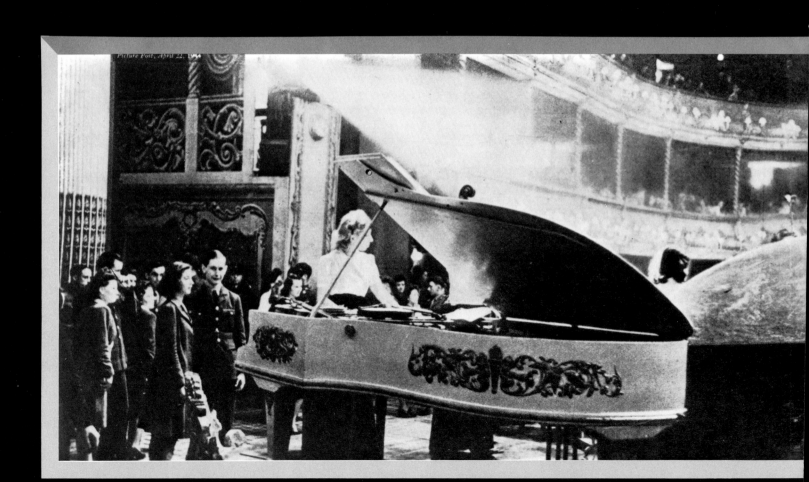
Picture Post, April 22, 19..

146 (PREVIOUS PAGE) COVENT GARDEN for the masses: the Mecca dance hall in the Second World War

147 ALAN GREEN'S wartime dance band in the Royal Opera House, Covent Garden, while it was being used as
a *palais de danse*

148 THE ROYAL FAMILY at the Gala re-opening of the Royal Opera House on 20 February 1946. King George VI was
accompanied by Queen Elizabeth, Princess Elizabeth (the present Queen) and Princess Margaret

149 THE FIRST operatic production produced after the Second World War: *The Fairy Queen* (Purcell). Constant Lambert conducted

150 MOIRA SHEARER, MARGOT FONTEYN and PAMELA MAY in the premiere of *Symphonic Variations*
(Franck) (choreographed by Frederick Ashton; designed by Sophie Fedorovitch), 1946

151 ANTON DOLIN and ALICIA MARKOVA in *The Sleeping Beauty* (Tchaikovsky), 1947

152 MARGOT FONTEYN and DAVID BLAIR in *The Sleeping Beauty* (Tchaikovsky) (choreographed by Petipa; designed by Oliver Messel), 1956

153 *The Magic Flute* (Mozart), performed on 20 March 1947. The scene is set in Pamina's boudoir. The production was conducted by Karl Rankl, produced by Malcolm Baker and designed by Oliver Messel

154 EDITH COATES in the title role of *Carmen* (Bizet) and KENNETH NEATE as Don José (1947). This was one of the first post-war productions: conducted by Reginald Goodall; produced by Henry Cass; designed by Edward Burra

155 DER ROSENKAVALIER (Richard Strauss), 24 April 1947, with Constance Shacklock as Anina, Hubert Norville as Valzacchi, and David Franklin as Baron Ochs. This, the fourth production to be added to the repertory of post-war Covent Garden, was conducted by Karl Rankl, produced by Joan Cross, with sets by Robin Ironside

156 A Scene from *Peter Grimes*
(Britten), first performed at Covent
Garden in November 1947 (conducted
by Karl Rankl; produced by
Tyrone Guthrie; designed by
Tanya Moiseivitch)

157 *Turandot* (Puccini), 1947. Eva
Turner first appeared at Covent Garden
with the Carl Rosa company in 1920,
and first sang the role of Turandot here
in 1928. Her last Covent Garden
performance in this role was in 1948

158 HANS HOTTER as Hans Sachs in *The Mastersingers*
(Wagner), 21 January 1948

159 SALVADOR DALI's set for *Salome* (Richard Strauss), 1949, in the
Peter Brook production, conducted by Karl Rankl

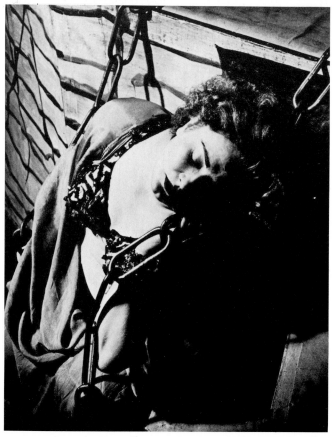

160 LJUBA WELITSCH as Salome, 1949

161 ELISABETH SCHWARZKOPF as Violetta in *La Traviata* (verdi) (conducted by
Reginald Goodall; produced by Tyrone Guthrie; designed by Sophie
Fedorovitch), 1948
Schwarzkopf was one of the great supports of the young Covent Garden
company, with her willingness to learn roles in English. She was married to
Walter Legge, who was associated with the theatre both before and after the war

162–163 TWO SUPREME BRÜNNHILDES

162 KIRSTEN FLAGSTAD (1895–1962), 1948

163 BIRGIT NILSSON, 1962

164 *Billy Budd* (Britten), 1951 (conducted by Benjamin Britten; produced by Basil Coleman; designed by John Piper)

165 DAVID TREE and JESS WALTERS in *Wozzeck* (Berg) (conducted by Erich Kleiber; produced by Sumner Austin; designed by Caspar Neher), 1952

166 *Orfeo* (Gluck) (conducted by John Barbirolli; produced by Frederick Ashton; designed by Sophie Fedorovitch). Kathleen Ferrier collapsed at the second performance of this production at Covent Garden on 6 February 1953 and never sang again

167 MARIA CALLAS (1923–77) and EBE STIGNANI
in *Norma* (Bellini) (conducted by Vittorio Gui; produced by
Gianfranco Enriques; designed by Alan Barlow), 1952

Ebe Stignani first appeared at Covent Garden in 1937 while this
was Maria Callas's Covent Garden debut

168 CALLAS AT COVENT GARDEN
Maria Callas as Norma, 1957

171 THE RITUAL DANCES in *The Midsummer Marriage* (Tippet) (conducted by John Pritchard; produced by Christopher West; designed by Barbara Hepworth) which was first performed on 27 January 1955

172 NADIA NERINA and DAVID BLAIR (1932–76) in *Coppélia* (Délibes) (choreographed by Cecchetti and Ivanov; designed by Osbert Lancaster), 1954

169 *Gloriana* (Britten) (conducted by John Pritchard; produced by Basil Coleman; designed by John Piper), performed at the Coronation Gala in June 1953. The audience was startled when Joan Cross as Queen Elizabeth I was revealed with a bald white head. The theatre was lavishly decorated by Oliver Messel

170 MARGOT FONTEYN in *Firebird* (Stravinsky) (choreographed by Mikhail Fokine; designed by Nathalie Goncharova), 1954

173 MARGOT FONTEYN with HM
The Queen and HRH the Duke of
Edinburgh at the Centenary Gala, 1958

174 THE CENTENARY GALA of the Royal
Opera House, 10 June 1958
The celebration of the opening of the
third theatre on the Covent Garden site
was held in the presence of
HM Queen Elizabeth II and
HRH the Duke of Edinburgh. The
performance included extracts from five
operas and one ballet

175 MARGOT FONTEYN in the Shadow Dance from *Ondine* (Henze)
(choreographed by Frederick Ashton; designed by Lila de Nobile), 1958

177 JOAN SUTHERLAND in *La Fille du Régiment* (Donizetti)
(conducted by Richard Bonynge; produced by Sandro Sequi;
designed by Anna Anni and Marcel Escoffier), 1966
A very light-hearted role, and a strong contrast to the intensity of
her Lucia

176 JOAN SUTHERLAND in
Lucia di Lammermoor (Donizetti)
(conducted by Tullio Serafin;
produced and designed by Franco
Zeffirelli), 17 February 1959

This role laid the foundation for her
spectacular career

178 DAVID WEBSTER (1903–71)
General Administrator for over a
quarter of a century, he piloted Covent
Garden through its early difficulties in
the immediate post-war years, and on
towards many fine productions and an
enviable international reputation. His
biographer described him as 'a
magnificent showman': he was very
much in the tradition of Frederick Gye
and Sir Augustus Harris. He was
knighted in 1961

179 GERDA LAMMERS as Kundry, in
the 1959 production of *Parsifal*
(Wagner) (conducted by Rudolf
Kempe; produced by Herbert Graf;
designed by Paul Walter). She had also
sung a powerful and exciting Elektra
two years before

181 *Fidelio* (Beethoven): Dr Klemperer
going over the score with Jon Vickers,
John Dobson, and, on his right, Sena
Jurinac, on his left, Elsie Morison,
22 February 1961

180 GERAINT EVANS in the title role
of *Falstaff* (Verdi) (conducted by Carlo
Maria Giulini; produced and designed
by Franco Zeffirelli), with Regina
Resnik as Mistress Quickly, 1961

182 (OVERLEAF) The corps de ballet in
La Bayadère (Minkus) (choreographed
by Petipa and Nureyev; designed by
Philip Prowse), 1963

183 MONICA MASON as The Chosen Maiden in *The Rite of Spring* (Stravinsky)
(choreographed by Kenneth MacMillan; designed by Sidney Nolan), 1962

184 AMY SHUARD in *Erwartung* (Schoenberg), 1962
This was the English premiere of Schoenberg's monodrama, in a production by
Peter Ustinov, with Georg Solti conducting

185 TITO GOBBI, GEORGE SOLTI and JOHN McCRACKEN during the
1963 revival of *Otello* (Verdi)

186 TITO GOBBI as Scarpia in *Tosca*
(Puccini), 1964

188 The memorable 1964 production of *Tosca* (Puccini). From left to right: Tito
Gobbi, Franco Zeffirelli, Maria Callas, Carlo Felice Cillario and Renato Cioni

187 MARIA CALLAS in the title role and TITO GOBBI as
Scarpia in *Tosca* (Puccini) (conducted by Carlo Felice Cillario;
produced by Franco Zeffirelli; designed by Renzo Mongiardino
and Marcel Escoffier), 1964

189 TITO GOBBI and BORIS CHRISTOFF in
Don Carlos (Verdi) (conducted by Carlo
Maria Giulini; designed and produced by
Luchino Visconti), 1958

190 MARIE COLLIER (1926–71) as Nedda and JOHN SHAW as
Tonio in *Pagliacci* (Leoncavallo) (conducted by Bryan Balkwell;
produced and designed by Franco Zeffirelli), 1965
Marie Collier's tragically early death cut short a brilliant career

191 FORBES ROBINSON as Moses and RICHARD LEWIS as
Aaron in the British premiere of *Moses und Aaron* (Schoenberg)
(conducted by Georg Solti; produced by Peter Hall; designed by
John Bury and Ann Curtis), 1965

192 ROBERT HELPMANN and FREDERICK ASHTON as the Ugly Sisters
in *Cinderella* (Prokofiev) (choreographed by Frederick Ashton; designed by Henry Bardon and
David Walker), 1965

193 ROBERT MEAD, VYVYAN LORRAYNE and ANTHONY DOWELL
in *Monotones* (Satie) (choreographed and designed by Frederick Ashton), 1965

194 DAME NINETTE DE VALOIS

195 BRONISLAVA NIJINSKA (1891–1972) (centre) with SVETLANA
BERIOSOVA and FREDERICK ASHTON at a rehearsal of *Les Noces*
(Stravinsky) (choreographed by Bronislava Nijinska designed by
Nathalie Goncharova), 1966

197 ANTOINETTE SIBLEY and ANTHONY DOWELL in *The Nutcracker*
(Tchaikovsky) (choreographed by Rudolf Nureyev; designed by
Nicholas Georgiadis), 1968

196 MONICA MASON and
ANTHONY DOWELL in
Song of the Earth (Mahler)
(choreographed by
Kenneth MacMillan), 1966

198 ANN JENNER as Lise and DAVID WALL as Colas in *La Fille mal gardée* (Hérold) (choreographed by Frederick Ashton; designed by Osbert Lancaster), 1967

199 THE FIRST Covent Garden production of *Die Frau ohne Schatten* (Richard Strauss) (conducted by George Solti; produced by Rudolf Hartmann; designed by Josef Svoboda and Carl Toms), 1967

200 GRACE BUMBRY as Amneris in *Aida* (Verdi) (conducted by Edward Downes;
produced by Peter Potter; designed by Nicholas Georgiadis), 1968

201 LISA DELLA CASA as the Marschallin and Yvonne Minton as Octavian in *Der Rosenkavalier* (Richard Strauss) (conducted by Silvio Vavviso; produced and designed by Luchino Visconti), 1968

202 *Enigma Variations* (Elgar) with SVETLANA BERIOSOVA and
DEREK RENCHER (choreographed by Frederick Ashton; designed by
Julia Trevelyan Oman), 1968

203 JOSEPHINE VEASEY as Dido in a new production of *Les
Troyens* (Berlioz) (conducted by Colin Davis; produced by Minos
Volanakis; designed by Nicholas Georgiadis), 1969

204 ELISABETH SÖDERSTRÖM as Mélisande in *Pelléas et
Mélisande* (Debussy) (conducted by Pierre Boulez; produced by
Vaclav Kaslik; designed by Josef Svoboda and Jan Skalicky), 1969

205 The Second Act of *Anastasia* (Tschaikovsky and Martinu) (choreographed by Kenneth MacMillan; designed by Barry Kay), 1971. Derek Rencher danced the part of the Czar, Svetlana Beriosova, the Czarina; Adrian Grater was the monk, Rasputin, and Antoinette Sibley the Czar's mistress, the dancer Kshessinska. The title role was danced by Lynn Seymour

207 DAVID WALL and LYNN SEYMOUR in *Romeo and Juliet* (Prokofiev) (choreographed by Kenneth MacMillan; designed by Nicholas Georgiadis), 1970

206 Act I Scene 1 of *Romeo and Juliet* (Prokofiev) (choreographed by Kenneth MacMillan; designed by Nicholas Georgiadis), 1971

208 A new production of *Così fan tutte*
(Mozart) (conducted by George Solti;
produced by John Copley; designed by
Henry Bardon and David Walker), 1968

209 *Swan Lake* (1971): ANTOINETTE SIBLEY and
ANTHONY DOWELL, a fine partnership frustrated by her
early retirement

210 A new production of *Le Nozze di Figaro* (Mozart) (conducted by
Colin Davis; produced by John Copley; designed by Stefan Lazaridis and
Michael Stennett), 1971

211 KIRI TE KANAWA as the
Countess in *Le Nozze di Figaro*
(Mozart), 1971

212 WORLD PREMIERE of *Taverner*
(Maxwell Davies) (conducted by
Edward Downs; produced by Michael
Geliot; designed by Ralph Koltai), 1972

214 JENNIFER PENNEY and WAYNE EAGLING in *Manon* (Massenet)
(choreographed by Kenneth MacMillan; designed by Nicholas Georgiadis), 1974

213 RUDOLF NUREYEV in *The
Prodigal Son* (Stravinsky) (choreographed
by George Balanchine; designed by
Georges Rouault), 1973

215 JANET BAKER as Vitellia in *La Clemenza di Tito* (Mozart) (conducted by Colin Davis; produced by Anthony Besch; designed by John Stoddart), 1974

216 MARGARET BARBIERI as The Betrayed Girl, STEPHEN JEFFERIES as The Rake in *The Rake's Progress* (Stravinsky) (choreographed by Ninette de Valois; designed by Rex Whistler), 1974

217 BORIS CHRISTOFF as Boris and ANNE PASHLEY as Feodor in
Boris Godunov (Mussorgsky) (conducted by Yuri Ahronovitch; produced by
Ande Anderson; designed by Georges Wakhevitch), 1974

218 ILEANA COTRUBAS and RICHARD STILWELL in *Pelléas et Mélisande*
(Debussy) (conducted by Colin Davis; produced by Vaclav Kaslik; designed by
Josef Svoboda and Jan Skalicky), 1974

219 *Carmen* (Bizet) with SHIRLEY VERRETT and PLACIDO
DOMINGO (conducted by Georg Solti; produced by Michael
Geliot; designed by Jenny Beavan), 1973

220 JON VICKERS in a new
production of *Peter Grimes* (Britten)
(conducted by Colin Davis; produced
by Elijah Moshinsky; designed by
Timothy O'Brien and Tazeena Firth),
1975

221 A Scene From *Benvenuto Cellini* (Berlioz) (conducted by Colin Davis; produced by John Copley; designed by Beni Montresor), 1976

222 World Premiere of Hans Werner Henze's *We Come to the River* (conducted by David Atherton; produced by Hans Werner Henze; designed by Jurgen Henze), 1976

224 *Die Walküre* with DONALD McINTYRE as Wotan and BERIT
LINDHOLME as Brünnhilde (conducted by Colin Davis; produced by Götz
Friedrich; designed by Josef Svoboda and Ingrid Rosell)

223–224 The *Ring* (Wagner) (1974–5)

223 THE final scene of *Das Rheingold*

225 ILEANA COTRUBAS as Adina and INGVAR WIXELL as Belcore in *L'Elisir d'Amore* (Donizetti) (conducted by John Pritchard; produced by John Copley; designed by Beni Montresor), 1976

226 LYNN SEYMOUR and ANTHONY DOWELL in *A Month in the Country* (Chopin) (choreographed by Frederick Ashton; designed by Julia Trevelyan Oman), 1976

227 LYNN SEYMOUR in the title role of *Manon* (Massenet) (choreographed by Kenneth MacMillan), 1977
With Christopher Gable, she was the inspiration for Kenneth MacMillan's *Romeo and Juliet*, although they did not dance the roles at the first performance

229 RUDOLF NUREYEV and MARGOT FONTEYN in
Marguerite and Armand (Liszt) (choreographed by Frederick
Ashton; designed by Cecil Beaton), 1963

228 LYNN SEYMOUR as The Girl and DESMOND KELLY as
The Husband in *The Invitation* (Seiber) (choreographed by
Kenneth MacMillan; designed by Nicholas Georgiadis), 1976

230 Robert Lloyd, Gerald English and
Janet Baker in *Troilus and Cressida*
(Walton) (conducted by Lawrence
Foster; produced by Colin Graham;
designed by Christopher Morley and
Ann Curtis), 1976

231 THE 1979 revival of *Die Fledermaus*
(Johann Strauss) (conducted by Peter
Maag; produced by
Leopold Lindtberg; designed by
Julia Trevelyan Oman)

232 Lucia Popp, Hannelore Bode, René Kollo, Richard Van Allan, and Donald McIntyre in the final scene of *Der Freischütz* (Weber) (conducted by Colin Davis; produced by Götz Friedrich; designed by Günther Schneider-Siemssen and Aliute Meczies), 1977

233 KATIA RICCIARELLI and LUCIANO PAVAROTTI in a new production of *Luisa Miller* (Verdi) (conducted by Lorin Maazel; produced and designed by Filippo Sanjust), 1978

234 YVONNE MINTON and PETER
HOFMANN in *Parsifal* (Wagner)
(conducted by Georg Solti; produced
by Terry Hands; designed by Farrah),
1979

235 MIRELLA FRENI as Mimi and
PETER DVORSKY as Rodolfo in
La Bohème (Puccini) (conducted by
Robin Stapleton; produced by
John Copley; designed by
Julia Trevelyan Oman), 1980

236 PLACIDO DOMINGO and SILVANO CARROLI in *Otello* (Verdi)
(conducted by Carlos Kleiber; designed by Georges Wakhevitch), 1980

238 TERESA BERGANZA and ALFREDO KRAUS in *Werther* (Massenet)
(conducted by Colin Davis; produced by John Copley; designed by Stefanos
Lazardis and Michael Stennett), 1980

237 THOMAS ALLEN as Papageno in *Die Zauberflöte* (Mozart)
(conducted by James Conlon; produced by August Everding;
designed by Jürgen Rose), 1980

240 KARAN ARMSTRONG in the title role with GUNTHER REICH as Dr Schön in Covent Garden's first production of *Lulu* (Berg) (conducted by Colin Davis; produced by Götz Friedrich; designed by Timothy O'Brien), 1981. The completed Third Act was included

239 JENNIFER PENNEY and JULIAN HOSKING in *Gloria* (Poulenc) (choreographed by Kenneth MacMillan; designed by Andy Klunder), first performed on 13 March 1980

241 MONTSERRAT CABALLÉ and LUCIANO PAVAROTTI in *Un Ballo in
Maschera* (Verdi) (conducted by Bernard Haitink; produced by Otto Schenk;
designed by Jürgen Rose), 1981

242 PLACIDO DOMINGO in the title role of a new production of *Les Contes d'Hoffman* (Offenbach) (conducted by George Prêtre; produced by John Schlesinger; designed by William Dudley and Maria Bjornson), 1980. Hoffman is seen here at the end of Act I distraught to find that his first love is no more than a mechanical doll

243 HRH The Prince of Wales, the Patron of the Royal Opera, making a
film in support of the Development Appeal, May 1979

244 HRH The Prince of Wales inspecting a model of the new extension to the theatre. With him is the General Director, Sir John Tooley

245 HRH The Duke of Edinburgh, HM
Queen Elizabeth The Queen Mother,
HM The Queen and HRH The Princess
Margaret, Countess of Snowdon,
President of The Royal Ballet, at a Gala
Tribute to The Queen Mother on her
80th birthday, 4 August 1980